ENERGY:
The World's Race for Resources in the 21st Century

Hardly anything is more explosive than the question of the energy supply of the future. Due to the population explosion, consumption is certain to increase dramatically, and the worldwide political structure will be reordered, due to the issue of resources. And we will also have to find alternative energy sources to avoid a climate catastrophe.

Hermann-Josef Wagner is a professor for energy systems and energy economy at the Ruhr-University of Bochum. He has studied the technical and economic issues involving today's energy supply and that of the future.

Our addresses on the Internet:
www.the-sustainability-project.com
www.forum-fuer-verantwortung.de
[English version available]

ENERGY:
The World's Race for Resources
in the 21st Century

HERMANN-JOSEF WAGNER

Translated by Phil Hill

Klaus Wiegandt, General Editor

HAUS PUBLISHING

First published in Great Britain in 2008 by
Haus Publishing Ltd
70 Cadogan Place
Draycott Avenue
London SW1X 9AH
www.hauspublishing.com

Originally published as: FORUM FÜR VERANTWORTUNG, *"Was sind die Energie des 21. Jahrhunderts?"*, by Hermann-Josef Wagner
Ed. by Klaus Wiegandt
© 2007 Fischer Taschenbuch Verlag in der S. Fischer Verlag GmbH, Frankfurt am Main

English translation copyright © Phil Hill 2008

The moral right of the author has been asserted

A CIP catalogue record for this book
is available from the British Library

ISBN 978-1-906598-08-2

Typeset in Sabon by MacGuru Ltd
Printed in Dubai by Oriental Press

Mixed Sources
Product group from well-managed forests and other controlled sources
www.fsc.org Cert no. CU-COC-809367
© 1996 Forest Stewardship Council

FSC

Haus Publishing believes in the importance of a sustainable future for our planet. This book is printed on paper produced in accordance with the standards of sustainability set out and monitored by the FSC. The printer holds chain of custody.

Contents

Editor's Foreword

Sustainability Project

Sales of the German-language edition of this series have exceeded all expectations. The positive media response has been encouraging, too. Both of these positive responses demonstrate that the series addresses the right topics in a language that is easily understood by the general reader. The combination of thematic breadth and scientifically astute, yet generally accessible writing, is particularly important as I believe it to be a vital prerequisite for smoothing the way to a sustainable society by turning knowledge into action. After all, I am not a scientist myself; my background is in business.

A few months ago, shortly after the first volumes had been published, we received suggestions from neighboring countries in Europe recommending that an English-language edition would reach a far larger readership. Books dealing with global challenges, they said, require global action brought about by informed debate amongst as large an audience as possible. When delegates from India, China, and Pakistan voiced similar concerns at an international conference my mind was made up. Dedicated individuals such as Lester R. Brown and Jonathan Porritt deserve credit for bringing the concept of sustainability to the attention of the general public, I am convinced that this series can give the discourse about sustainability something new.

Two years have passed since I wrote the foreword to the initial German edition. During this time, unsustainable developments on our planet have come to our attention in ever more dramatic ways. The price of oil has nearly tripled; the value of industrial metals has risen exponentially and, quite unexpectedly, the costs of staple foods such as corn, rice, and wheat have reached all-time highs. Around the globe, people are increasingly concerned that the pressure caused by these drastic price increases will lead to serious destabilization in China, India, Indonesia, Vietnam, and Malaysia, the world's key developing regions.

The frequency and intensity of natural disasters brought on by global warming has continued to increase. Many regions of our Earth are experiencing prolonged droughts, with subsequent shortages of drinking water and the destruction of entire harvests. In other parts of the world, typhoons and hurricanes are causing massive flooding and inflicting immeasurable suffering.

The turbulence in the world's financial markets, triggered by the US sub-prime mortgage crisis, has only added to these woes. It has affected every country and made clear just how unscrupulous and sometimes irresponsible speculation has become in today's financial world. The expectation of exorbitant short-term rates of return on capital investments led to complex and obscure financial engineering. Coupled with a reckless willingness to take risks everyone involved seemingly lost track of the situation. How else can blue chip companies incur multi-billion dollar losses? If central banks had not come to the rescue with dramatic steps to back up their currencies, the world's economy would have collapsed. It was only in these circumstances that the use of public monies could be justified. It is therefore imperative to prevent a repeat of speculation with short-term capital on such a gigantic scale.

Taken together, these developments have at least significantly improved the readiness for a debate on sustainability. Many more are now aware that our wasteful use of natural resources and energy have serious consequences, and not only for future generations.

Two years ago, who would have dared to hope that WalMart, the world's largest retailer, would initiate a dialog about sustainability with its customers and promise to put the results into practice? Who would have considered it possible that CNN would start a series "Going Green"? Every day, more and more businesses worldwide announce that they are putting the topic of sustainability at the core of their strategic considerations. Let us use this momentum to try and make sure that these positive developments are not a flash in the pan, but a solid part of our necessary discourse within civic society.

However, we cannot achieve sustainable development through a multitude of individual adjustments. We are facing the challenge of critical fundamental questioning of our lifestyle and consumption and patterns of production. We must grapple with the complexity of the entire earth system in a forward-looking and precautionary manner, and not focus solely on topics such as energy and climate change.

The authors of these twelve books examine the consequences of our destructive interference in the Earth ecosystem from different perspectives. They point out that we still have plenty of opportunities to shape a sustainable future. If we want to achieve this, however, it is imperative that we use the information we have as a basis for systematic action, guided by the principles of sustainable development. If the step from knowledge to action is not only to be taken, but also to succeed, we need to offer comprehensive education to all, with the foundation in early childhood. The central issues of the future must be anchored firmly in school curricula, and no university student should be permitted to graduate without having completed a general course on sustainable development. Everyday opportunities for action must be made clear to us all – young and old. Only then can we begin to think critically about our lifestyles and make positive changes in the direction of sustainability. We need to show the business community the way to sustainable development via a responsible attitude to consumption, and become active within our sphere of influence as opinion leaders.

For this reason, my foundation *Forum für Verantwortung*, the ASKO EUROPA-FOUNDATION, and the European Academy Otzenhausen have joined forces to produce educational materials on the future of the Earth to accompany the twelve books developed at the renowned Wuppertal Institute for Climate, Environment and Energy. We are setting up an extensive program of seminars, and the initial results are very promising. The success of our initiative "Encouraging Sustainability," which has now been awarded the status of an official project of the UN Decade "Education for Sustainable Development," confirms the public's great interest in, and demand for, well-founded information.

I would like to thank the authors for their additional effort to update all their information and put the contents of their original volumes in a more global context. My special thanks goes to the translators, who submitted themselves to a strict timetable, and to Annette Maas for coordinating the Sustainability Project. I am grateful for the expert editorial advice of Amy Irvine and the Haus Publishing editorial team for not losing track of the "3600-page-work."

Taking Action — Out of Insight and Responsibility

"We were on our way to becoming gods, supreme beings who could create a second world, using the natural world only as building blocks for our new creation."

This warning by the psychoanalyst and social philosopher Erich Fromm is to be found in *To Have or to Be?* (1976). It aptly expresses the dilemma in which we find ourselves as a result of our scientific-technical orientation.

The original intention of submitting to nature in order to make use of it ("knowledge is power") evolved into subjugating nature in order to exploit it. We have left the earlier successful path with its many advances and are now on the wrong track, a path of danger with incalculable risks. The greatest danger stems from the unshakable faith of the overwhelming majority of politicians and business leaders in unlimited economic growth which, together with limitless technological innovation, is supposed to provide solutions to all the challenges of the present and the future.

For decades now, scientists have been warning of this collision course with nature. As early as 1983, the United Nations founded the World Commission on Environment and Development which published the Brundtland Report in 1987. Under the title *Our Common Future*, it presented a concept that could save mankind from catastrophe and help to find the way back to a responsible way of life, the concept of long-term environmentally sustainable use of resources. "Sustainability," as used in the Brundtland Report, means "development that meets the needs of the present without compromising the ability of future generations to meet their own needs."

Despite many efforts, this guiding principle for ecologically, economically, and socially sustainable action has unfortunately not yet become the reality it can, indeed must, become. I believe the reason for this is that civil societies have not yet been sufficiently informed and mobilized.

Forum für Verantwortung

Against this background, and in the light of ever more warnings and scientific results, I decided to take on a societal responsibility with my foundation. I would like to contribute to the expansion of public discourse about sustainable development which is absolutely essential. It is my desire to provide a large number of people with facts and contextual knowledge on the subject of sustainability, and to show alternative options for future action.

After all, the principle of "sustainable development" alone is insufficient to change current patterns of living and economic practices. It does provide some orientation, but it has to be negotiated in concrete terms within society and then implemented in patterns of behavior. A democratic society seriously seeking to reorient itself towards future viability must rely on critical, creative individuals capable of both discussion and action. For this reason, life-long learning, from childhood to old age, is a necessary precondition for realizing sustainable development. The practical implementation of the ecological, economic, and social goals of a sustainability strategy in economic policy requires people able to reflect, innovate and recognize potentials for structural change and learn to use them in the best interests of society.

It is not enough for individuals to be merely "concerned." On the contrary, it is necessary to understand the scientific background and interconnections in order to have access to them and be able to develop them in discussions that lead in the right direction. Only in this way can the ability to make appropriate judgments emerge, and this is a prerequisite for responsible action.

The essential condition for this is presentation of both the facts and the theories within whose framework possible courses of action are visible in a manner that is both appropriate to the subject matter and comprehensible. Then, people will be able to use them to guide their personal behavior.

In order to move towards this goal, I asked renowned scientists to present in a generally understandable way the state of research and the possible options on twelve important topics in the area of sustainable development in the series *"Forum für Verantwortung."* All those involved in this project are in agreement that there is no alternative to a united path of all societies towards sustainability:

- *Our Planet: How Much More Can Earth Take?* (Jill Jäger)
- *Our Threatened Oceans* (Stefan Rahmstorf and Katherine Richardson)
- *Water Resources: Efficient, Sustainable and Equitable Use* (Wolfgang Mauser)
- *Energy: The World's Race for Resources in the 21st Century* (Hermann-Joseph Wagner)
- *The Earth: Natural Resources and Human Intervention* (Friedrich Schmidt-Bleek)
- *Overcrowded World? Global Population and International Migration* (Rainer Münz and Albert F. Reiterer)
- *Feeding the Planet: Environmental Protection through Sustainable Agriculture* (Klaus Hahlbrock)
- *Costing the Earth? Perspectives of Sustainable Development* (Bernd Meyer)

The public debate

What gives me the courage to carry out this project and the optimism that I will reach civil societies in this way, and possibly provide an impetus for change?

For one thing, I have observed that, because of the number and severity of natural disasters in recent years, people have become more sensitive concerning questions of how we treat the Earth. For another, there are scarcely any books on the market that cover in language comprehensible to civil society the broad spectrum of comprehensive sustainable development in an integrated manner.

When I began to structure my ideas and the prerequisites for a public discourse on sustainability in 2004, I could not foresee that by the time the first books of the series were published, the general public would have come to perceive at least climate change and energy as topics of great concern. I believe this occurred especially as a result of the following events:

First, the United States witnessed the devastation of New Orleans in August 2005 by Hurricane Katrina, and the anarchy following in the wake of this disaster.

Second, in 2006, Al Gore began his information campaign on

climate change and wastage of energy, culminating in his film *An Inconvenient Truth*, which has made an impression on a wide audience of all age groups around the world.

Third, the 700-page Stern Report, commissioned by the British government, published in 2007 by the former Chief Economist of the World Bank Nicholas Stern in collaboration with other economists, was a wake-up call for politicians and business leaders alike. This report makes clear how extensive the damage to the global economy will be if we continue with "business as usual" and do not take vigorous steps to halt climate change. At the same time, the report demonstrates that we could finance countermeasures for just one-tenth of the cost of the probable damage, and could limit average global warming to 2° C – if we only took action.

Fourth, the most recent IPCC report, published in early 2007, was met by especially intense media interest, and therefore also received considerable public attention. It laid bare as never before how serious the situation is, and called for drastic action against climate change.

Last, but not least, the exceptional commitment of a number of billionaires such as Bill Gates, Warren Buffett, George Soros, and Richard Branson as well as Bill Clinton's work to "save the world" is impressing people around the globe and deserves mention here.

An important task for the authors of our twelve-volume series was to provide appropriate steps towards sustainable development in their particular subject area. In this context, we must always be aware that successful transition to this type of economic, ecological, and social development on our planet cannot succeed immediately, but will require many decades. Today, there are still no sure formulae for the most successful long-term path. A large number of scientists and even more innovative entrepreneurs and managers will have to use their creativity and dynamism to solve the great challenges. Nonetheless, even today, we can discern the first clear goals we must reach in order to avert a looming catastrophe. And billions of consumers around the world can use their daily purchasing decisions to help both ease and significantly accelerate the economy's transition to sustainable development – provided the political framework is there. In addition, from a global perspective, billions of citizens have the opportunity to mark out the political "guide rails" in a democratic way via their parliaments.

The most important insight currently shared by the scientific, political, and economic communities is that our resource-intensive Western model of prosperity (enjoyed today by one billion people) cannot be extended to another five billion or, by 2050, at least eight billion people. That would go far beyond the biophysical capacity of the planet. This realization is not in dispute. At issue, however, are the consequences we need to draw from it.

If we want to avoid serious conflicts between nations, the industrialized countries must reduce their consumption of resources by more than the developing and threshold countries increase theirs. In the future, all countries must achieve the same level of consumption. Only then will we be able to create the necessary ecological room for maneuver in order to ensure an appropriate level of prosperity for developing and threshold countries.

To avoid a dramatic loss of prosperity in the West during this long-term process of adaptation, the transition from high to low resource use, that is, to an ecological market economy, must be set in motion quickly.

On the other hand, the threshold and developing countries must commit themselves to getting their population growth under control within the foreseeable future. The twenty-year

Programme of Action adopted by the United Nations International Conference on Population and Development in Cairo in 1994 must be implemented with stronger support from the industrialized nations.

If humankind does not succeed in drastically improving resource and energy efficiency and reducing population growth in a sustainable manner – we should remind ourselves of the United Nations forecast that population growth will come to a halt only at the end of this century, with a world population of eleven to twelve billion – then we run the real risk of developing eco-dictatorships. In the words of Ernst Ulrich von Weizsäcker: "States will be sorely tempted to ration limited resources, to micromanage economic activity, and in the interest of the environment to specify from above what citizens may or may not do. 'Quality-of-life' experts might define in an authoritarian way what kind of needs people are permitted to satisfy." (*Earth Politics*, 1989, in English translation: 1994).

It is time

It is time for us to take stock in a fundamental and critical way. We, the public, must decide what kind of future we want. Progress and quality of life is not dependent on year-by-year growth in per capita income alone, nor do we need inexorably growing amounts of goods to satisfy our needs. The short-term goals of our economy, such as maximizing profits and accumulating capital, are major obstacles to sustainable development. We should go back to a more decentralized economy and reduce world trade and the waste of energy associated with it in a targeted fashion. If resources and energy were to cost their "true" prices, the global process of rationalization and labor displacement will be reversed, because cost pressure will be shifted to the areas of materials and energy.

The path to sustainability requires enormous technological innovations. But not everything that is technologically possible has to be put into practice. We should not strive to place all areas of our lives under the dictates of the economic system. Making justice and fairness a reality for everyone is not only a moral and ethical imperative, but is also the most important means of securing world peace in the long term. For this reason, it is essential to place the political relationship between states and peoples on a new basis, a basis with which everyone can identify, not only the most powerful. Without common principles of global governance, sustainability cannot become a reality in any of the fields discussed in this series.

And finally, we must ask whether we humans have the right to reproduce to such an extent that we may reach a population of eleven to twelve billion by the end of this century, laying claim to every square centimeter of our Earth and restricting and destroying the habitats and way of life of all other species to an ever greater degree.

Our future is not predetermined. We ourselves shape it by our actions. We can continue as before, but if we do so, we will put ourselves in the biophysical straitjacket of nature, with possibly disastrous political implications, by the middle of this century. But we also have the opportunity to create a fairer and more viable future for ourselves and for future generations. This requires the commitment of everyone on our planet.

Klaus Wiegandt
Summer 2008

Foreword

Not a week goes by without some report in the daily press about uncertainties of energy supply and rising prices of energy. Energy has become a daily topic. Many suggestions have been presented as to how energy could be saved, or how additional alternative energies could make a contribution.

What is missing is a sober presentation of the facts permitting a comparative classification of the various problems. This book is designed to fill that gap. Starting with a discussion of the various forms of energy, it describes the supply and consumption situation worldwide. It deals with questions of access to deposit areas and addresses the conflicts between energy consumption and sustainable development.

My argument proceeds at three levels: first, from the point of view of the disequilibrium in energy consumption and population growth between the rich and poor countries in the world; second from the viewpoint of energy supply and consumption in an industrial country, e.g. in Germany; and finally from the view of individual energy needs. This is designed to provide an adequately holistic view of energy problems.

In this book, I will try to describe all important developments and effects in their complete context. However, it is impossible, in the context of such a book, to address every technological or economic option existing or conceivable in the future.

This book, like the entire series on the future of humankind, has been initiated by Mr. Klaus Wiegandt, founder and chairman of the Forum für Verantwortung (Forum for Responsibility). Mr. Wiegandt deserves sincere thanks for his dedication to addressing the issues of the future of humankind.

It was only possible to write this book with the help of Ms. Stefanie Weber and particularly from Ms. Manuela Kötter. I would like here to express my heartfelt gratitude for their writing work, their suggestions and their critical remarks on several of the issues.

I would like to thank Mr. Phil Hill very much for his comments and for the translation of this book from German into English.

Hermann-Josef Wagner

The Different Faces of Energy

1 The Forms and Units of Energy

Energy is familiar to all of us in our everyday lives: electric power, gas and gasoline. In school, we have learned that there are electrical, mechanical and other forms of energy. Energy occurs and can be used in many forms:

- potential energy obtained through a difference in altitude – such as hydroelectric power
- kinetic energy through moving particles – such as wind power
- chemical energy – such as the energy stored in coal
- thermal energy – such as the heat from burning coal
- electrical energy – the electric power in the grid
- electromagnetic energy – such as microwaves
- nuclear energy – both from nuclear fission and nuclear fusion.

Energy is the ability of a "system" to do work. Energy can be transferred from one system to another in any of three ways:

- by carrying out mechanical work, as in a belt drive
- by heat exchange, as in a steam engine
- by electromagnetic fields, as in an electromotor.

Physically speaking, energy can be converted from one form to another. Of particular practical importance are thermal and electrical energy.

The major share of the energy requirements of the world's people is today met by energy sources which are burned and produce heat – or thermal energy. According to the laws of physics, only part of heat energy generated can ever be converted into mechanical energy. This share is greater, the higher the top process temperature and the lower the bottom process temperature of the combustion process is. The top process temperature is generally restricted by the material features of the facility, the bottom process temperature by the temperature of the environment. This process permits mechanical energy to be converted into electric power.

That heat energy which is not converted must be passed on to the environment as waste heat if it cannot be otherwise used, for example for heating purposes. These factors are the reason, for example, that only 45% of the coal used can be converted into electricity, even in the most modern steam-driven power plants. The rest of the energy is passed on to the environment by way of cooling towers.

By comparison with thermal energy, electrical energy is very valuable, since it can be converted into all other forms of energy with no major loss; moreover, it is easily transportable by means of metal transmission lines.

Although energy can be neither "created" nor "destroyed" according to the laws of physics, but only converted from one form to another, we usually use the terms "energy generation" and "energy consumption," both in everyday life and in the energy industry. Economically, what is involved is indeed the relationship between producers and consumers. Energy that has been "used" is in fact economically worthless. We will therefore use these terms in this book, too.

1.1 The Energy Chain

The energy which humans use comes from *primary energy sources*. These are the energy sources which occur in nature: the fossil resources hard coal, brown coal, petroleum and natural gas, the nuclear fuels uranium and thorium, and the renewable energy sources biomass, sunlight, wind, hydroelectric power, geothermal energy and tidal energy. In most cases, these primary energy sources cannot be used directly. They are therefore for the most part converted into secondary energy sources (Fig. 1), such as coke, briquettes, fuel oil, gasoline, electric power or district heat. Secondary energy sources, such as fuel oil and gasoline, are standardized with regard to their chemical properties, and electric power with regard to its physical properties – what comes out of the pump is always the same mix of chemicals, and your outlet always delivers the same voltage and frequency. In some cases, secondary energy sources are even converted again, for example, heavy fuel oil also is used for power generation.

The secondary energy sources are transported to the "consumers," who use them. In energy statistics, they are then described as useful energy.

The consumers – private homes, retailers, commercial enterprises, industry, transportation – ultimately need *useful energy* in the form of space heat, hot water, a hot stove eye, light, refrigeration, the mechanical propulsion of engines, sound, etc.

Every transformation involves "losses" due to technical and often, too, for physical reasons, so that in Germany, for example, with today's technology, only about one third of the primary energy used is actually available as useful energy, on average.

The real engine driving energy use is people, and their need for food, warm rooms and comfort, the amount of which depends on

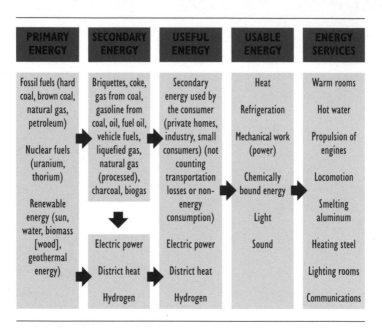

PRIMARY ENERGY	SECONDARY ENERGY	USEFUL ENERGY	USABLE ENERGY	ENERGY SERVICES
Fossil fuels (hard coal, brown coal, natural gas, petroleum)	Briquettes, coke, gas from coal, gasoline from coal, oil, fuel oil, vehicle fuels, liquefied gas, natural gas (processed), charcoal, biogas	Secondary energy used by the consumer (private homes, industry, small consumers) (not counting transportation losses or non-energy consumption)	Heat	Warm rooms
Nuclear fuels (uranium, thorium)			Refrigeration	Hot water
			Mechanical work (power)	Propulsion of engines
Renewable energy (sun, water, biomass [wood], geothermal energy)			Chemically bound energy	Locomotion
			Light	Smelting aluminum
	Electric power	Electric power	Sound	Heating steel
	District heat	District heat		Lighting rooms
	Hydrogen	Hydrogen		Communications

Figure 1 Types of energy: From primary energy to the factors which determine energy demand

their respective standard of living and economic activity. These amounts determine the so-called energy services, such as

- the volume of space to be heated or cooled to a given temperature level
- movement from one place to another at a certain speed (by car, train, etc.)
- the brightness and size of areas to be illuminated
- the quantities of aluminum, iron, copper, etc., to be melted (i.e., the production process).

The analysis of energy chains here has already recognized two substantial possibilities for action to reduce energy-related environmental impacts:

- If we reduce the factors which determine energy demand – such as by turning down the heat in our homes, driving fewer miles, or heating less space – we will need less energy at all levels, and can therefore reduce the associated ecological damage.
- Technology offers various chains to satisfy the same requirement for useful energy. For example, the useful energy for a given quantity of space heat may be provided either by electric storage heating with electric power from a brown coal power station (energy chain: brown coal – electric power – space heat), or by gas heat (energy chain: raw natural gas – processed natural gas – space heat). In the second case, the energy loss is less than in the first.

There are also possibilities for satisfying useful-energy requirements at different levels, with the same demand-defining factors. This applies particularly to space heating and cooling, where better or poorer insulation can increase or reduce heat loss, so that different amounts of useful energy are needed to warm or cool a room to a certain temperature.

1.2 Energy Units

The energy industry and energy technology commonly use a large number of energy units, which very frequently makes comparison of different data on energy consumption, energy requirements and types of energy sources difficult. To provide some

Prefixes for units and abbreviations			
kilo -	K	10^3	thousand
mega-	M	10^6	million
giga-	G	10^9	billion
tera-	T	10^{12}	trillion
peta-	P	10^{15}	quadrillion
exa-	E	10^{18}	quintillion

1 US (fluid) gallon = 3.79 liters
1 bbl (oil barrel) = 159 liters
1 million bbl/day = 50 million t/yr.
1 British thermal
unit (BTU) = 1.055 kJ

Conversion factors				
Unit	MJ	kWh	TCE	TOE
1 megajoule (MJ)	–	0.000278	0.000034	0.000024
1 kilowatt hour (kWh)	3.6	–	0.000123	0.000086
1 ton coal unit (TCE)	29,308	8,140	–	0.7
1 ton crude oil unit (TOE)	41,868	11,630	1.429	–

Table 1 Conversion of energy units (see text for abbreviations).

clarity, Table 1 contains a list of frequently used units, prefixes and conversion factors.

Although under the international unit system (SI) introduced in 1960, the joule (J) and the kilowatt hour (kWh) derived from it are the mandatory legal units for energy, the units "tons of coal equivalent" (TCE) and "tons of oil equivalent" (TOE) are still very frequently used in practice, because of their perceptual clarity. For example, one TCE is the quantity of energy contained in one ton of hard coal, and one TOE is the quantity of energy released by burning one ton of crude oil of a certain fixed brand. In the oil industry, the "barrel" (bbl or B), a standardized container for shipping oil, is also used worldwide as a unit of measure.

The unit of power in the SI unit system is the watt. The power of light bulbs is measured in watts (W), that of cars in kilowatts (kW, or 1000 watts), and of power stations in megawatts (MW, or 1,000,000 watts). In thermal power stations, the distinction is made between the *thermal output,* which represents the energy content of the steam at the time of entry into the turbine, and the *power output*, which is produced by the generator. The units MW_{th} for thermal output and MW_e for electrical output are often used to describe these two quantities of energy.

The electric-power consumption in a home is indicated in kilowatt hours (kWh). For example, a PC with a printer which runs for seven hours consumes one kWh, and a household uses between 3000 and 6000 kWh per year. On the other hand, the electric-power generation of a country is measured in terawatt-hours (TWh) – 1 billion kilowatt hours equal one terawatt-hour.

If we start to talk about the total primary energy consumption of a country or of the world, we need even larger units, for example petajoules (PJ) or exajoules (EJ). A petajoule is one quadrillion joules – a one with fifteen zeros, and an exajoule, or a quintillion joules, comes to eighteen zeros. These inconceivably large figures are due to the fact that a joule is an extremely small quantity of energy. One kWh of electric power, for example, already converts to 3,600,000 joules or 3.6 megajoules (MJ).

The joule is also familiar in everyday life, from nutrition tables. The daily consumption of food required by an adult person corresponds to about 7000 to 10,000 kilojoules of energy (erroneously, the "kilo" is often left out). Converted to other energy units, 10,000 kJ corresponds to approx. 2.8 kWh, or the heating value of approx. 0.28 liters (half a pint) of fuel oil. But of course, there's more to eating than just energy conversion.

In this book, various energy units are used, sometimes at the same time. Since the energy units joules and kilowatt hours are not very illustrative, we will more frequently describe energy quantities in TOE or in liters of crude oil, so that energy consumption can be visualized better. For instance, when referring to "tons of coal equivalent," you may think of a tractor-trailer truck which can haul a cargo of about fifteen tons. By the same token, "tons of oil equivalent" may let you imagine a similarly large tanker truck with a load volume of about 21,000 liters of oil weighing about eighteen tons.

2 Nature's Energy Supply

Historically, humankind originally used renewable energies. Many centuries before Christ, they were already being used to drive ships, windmills and waterwheels. The wind and the water provided mechanical energy. The heat energy came either directly from the sun, or else by burning wood which had grown thanks to solar energy. The growing population and their sedentary lifestyle were the reason why the energy source wood was already scarce in some parts of Central Europe during the Middle Ages. Hard coal was known in England from the 9th century, but the quantities mined with the production technology of the day were small. Together with pioneering developments in energy technology, such as the invention of the steam engine in 1769 or, later, the electric generator, completely new worlds opened up for the mechanization of production, and also of mobility. Hard coal and also ores could now be mined in large quantities.

People's living standards increased markedly. Only later did petroleum begin to attract their attention – but once it did, it rapidly developed into the most important energy source for the supply of energy to humankind, thanks to its characteristics, and it has stayed so to this day. Natural gas and nuclear energy are even more recent additions to the list of energy sources.

Wood and peat are no longer important factors in the energy supply picture of industrialized countries today. However, wood is still an important energy source for the rural population in

poor developing countries, and to some extent, it is traded commercially by merchants. It is used particularly for cooking. Generally, more wood is used than grows back. This often leads to
disastrous consequences for the environment: the deserts are
spreading into neighboring areas, for example into the Sahel
zone in Africa, because shrubbery which should hold back their
spread has been cut down. In Madagascar for example, the
monsoon rains wash the soil off the slopes, so that reforestation
is no longer possible. There are no official statistics on wood use,
but wood still provides around 5% of total worldwide energy
consumption, according to estimates.

In this chapter, we will briefly describe the various energy
forms which occur in nature, and how they are obtained and
transformed into usable energy sources. The purpose of this
description is to convey a feeling for the technical effort, the environmental impacts and the economic and political side-effects
that are involved in securing and processing these resources.

2.1 Coal

Coal occurs in different qualities, depending on the age of its
location. Very roughly, two major categories can be distin-
guished: brown coal and hard coal. Brown coal, so called for
its brownish color, is the geologically younger form of coal,
and it is found only a few countries in the world. One of them
is Germany, with its major brown-coal deposits in the Rhineland between Cologne and Aachen, in Lusatia southeast of
Berlin, and in central Germany, northwest of Leipzig. Depending on the site, brown coal may be up to 150 meters below the
earth's surface. Since the brown coal deposits are located in
densely populated areas, opening up of new strip mines means

relocating people. The soil above the coal, the so-called over-burden, must first be moved aside in order to mine the brown coal with large excavators up to 200 meters long and 150 meters high. The mining debris is then either transported to an adjacent, mined-out brown-coal pit, or else piled high into an artificial hill near the strip mine. An example is a stately hill which has arisen almost 200 meters above the landscape in the Rhineland near Jülich, next to Europe's largest brown-coal strip mine. To make sure water is kept out of the pit during operations, the groundwater must be pumped off from a large surrounding area, causing a crater-shaped drop in the ground-water level around the mine. Brown coal has low heating value and high water content, which can even cause conveyor belts and loads in railroad freight cars to freeze in winter, so that long hauls are economically inadvisable. For that reason, brown coal is for the most part moved by conveyor belts directly out of the strip mines to nearby power stations – the sites of which have thus been determined by the locations of the brown-coal deposits. Happily, these so-called seams are very thick, up to seventy meters, so that mining with large excavators is worthwhile. All in all, brown coal is a very favorable energy source from the point of view of cost. If parts of a deposit are mined out, the overburden over the remaining coal is dumped there, i.e., it is moved from one place to another within the same strip mine. Once it is completely mined out, the abandoned pit is normally turned into a lake for recreational purposes.

Brown coal is not processed further before it is burned in the power station furnaces. In the past, some of it was reprocessed to briquettes which were used for home heating and in industry, but since coal no longer accounts for any major share of the home heating market, briquette production has also declined considerably.

Hard coal is the older form of coal. It occurs in various types with various characteristics. Its heating value is approximately 2.5 times higher than that of brown coal, on average. For geological reasons, the world's coal stocks are very different with regard to their accessibility. Coal deposits comparable to German brown coal deposits in terms of size and seam thickness exist in the USA and Australia. They are therefore also strip-mined with large excavators. Such imported hard coal can be offered on the European market considerably more cheaply than locally-mined hard coal, the unmined deposits of which are 800 to 1700 meters underground, with seam thicknesses of only a few meters – often at such an incline that they are difficult to mine with mechanical equipment. Thanks to a high degree of mechanization in hard-coal mining in Germany, high outputs could be obtained and the higher labor costs partially compensated. Nevertheless, coal produced under such conditions is necessarily more expensive than imported coal, and is thus subsidized, which leads to permanent political pressure on the hard-coal mining industry. During the 1950s, 150 million tons of hard coal were still mined in Germany every year; by 2005, that had dropped to only 26 million tons, and the long-term policy goal is to phase out hard-coal mining in Germany altogether.

One example of a way to mine coal is with a so-called coal plow. Two parallel galleries about 100 meters apart are driven into the coal deposit area and connected by a crosscut in which the coal plow is installed. It looks almost like a large hand with pointed steel fingers, which are pulled by a chain and scrape the coal off. The coal falls onto a conveyor belt, which then transports it up to the shaft, where it is loaded onto cars for transportation to the surface. One use of hard coal is in power stations, another is as a refined product in the form of coke or coke coal, for steelmaking. In the past, the so-called town gas was obtained and used for heating in coke production. Today, it has been replaced by natural gas.

Since the geology of Central Europe provides for conditions considerably less favorable for coal mining than those in other coal deposits around the world, a number of European countries gave up or greatly reduced their hard-coal mining industry some two decades ago: Belgium and the Netherlands have completely abandoned their hard-coal mining operations, and Great Britain, Germany and Poland are in the process of reducing.

Both brown coal and hard coal contain sulfur, which, when burned, forms polluting sulfur dioxide. In modern power stations, this is removed from the flue gases via a chemical process.

2.2 Oil

Oil deposits are accessible both on land and offshore, by means of drilling platforms.

Petroleum is located in the pores of sand or rock formations, at depths up to about 3000 meters. Very frequently, petroleum deposits also contain gaseous hydrocarbons, which build up pressure in the deposit area, in addition to the pressure of the rock and soil. If the deposit is drilled into, the pressure in the deposit area forces the petroleum to the surface. This is known as *primary recovery*. Most oil fields producing today operate according to this method. If the pressure in the deposit area has dropped, or is too low due to natural conditions, artificial pressure will be required. This can be done by pumping in steam or carbon dioxide (CO_2), which is then called *secondary recovery*. If chemicals are also added to improve the possibility of recovery by reducing the viscosity of the oil, the term *tertiary* or *enhanced recovery* is used. On average, primary recovery can usually extract only about 25% of the oil physically present in the deposit areas, i.e. most of the oil stays in the ground. The degree of primary recovery of oil varies widely. In particularly favorable cases, it may amount to 40%; in unfavorable cases (little soil pressure, high viscosity of the petroleum), it may not even exceed 10%. With secondary and tertiary recovery, the degrees of oil extraction can be extended to up to 45% on average, i.e., it is possible to ultimately extract about 30% more oil from the deposit area, over and above the yield from primary recovery.

Chemically speaking, the different types of petroleum are a complex mixture of various hydrocarbons of different molecular sizes. They are predominantly chain-shaped (so-called paraffins) or also ring-shaped, like the naphthenes and aromatics. The higher the share of longer chains, the heavier the specific weight of the petroleum, and the greater the processing effort will be to obtain the light products demanded by the market. Highly in demand – and hence, higher-priced on the world market – are so-called light crude oils, for example Brent quality from the North Sea, or the Arabian Light specifications from Saudi Arabia. Heavy oils, such as that from Venezuela, are less popular. The technically utilizable features of newly extracted petroleum, or crude oil, are low; John D. Rockefeller is said to have remarked that it couldn't even be used to lubricate cart wheels. Only the products of the crude oil that emerge from the refinery can be used commercially. The refining process essentially consists of three stages. In the first, the distillation unit, the various chains are separated by heating, and achieve a specific temperature stratification in the fractionating column. So-called light, medium and heavy fractions are formed. As large a share as possible of the light fractions is desirable, since they are processed into the products which are most in demand on the market, such as aviation fuel, gasoline for cars, or raw materials for the chemical industry.

In the second step, the share of heavy fractions is reduced. The remaining long chains are broken down by pressure and temperature, hydrogen is added, and new, shorter chains, i.e., lighter fractions, are formed. In the third processing step, the individual products are refined to the market quality which must be guaranteed according to international standards, so that, for example, gasoline has the same quality at every pump.

For technical reasons, it is never possible to convert all heavy products into light or medium-weight ones, such as fuel oil or diesel oils. A modern refinery can therefore produce about 300 kg of light products, about 400 kg of medium products and about 300 kg of heavy products from a barrel of crude oil. The heavy fuel oil is frequently used as fuel for electric-power generation or for firing processes in factories. At room temperature, it is as thick as syrup and must be heated to over 100° C so that it can be pumped. Like hard coal, crude oil also contains sulfur, the proportions varying according to the origin of the oil. If it is still contained in the refined products, it will burn to sulfur dioxide (SO_2), and will then have to be separated out of the flue gases in a desulfurization scrubber. Another possibility is to immediately remove the sulfur from the crude oil in the refinery, with the aid of hydrogen. This process is used, for example, for the light fuel oil delivered to households, and for the diesel oils used in transportation.

In addition to the types of deposits described above, there are also major deposits of oil in the form of oil shale and oil sands in various parts of the world – as the name implies, these are sand and shale formations soaked with heavy oil. To recover the oil, they have to be mined, and then the oil extracted with the aid of heat. Another method is so-called *in-situ* gasification, by means of which the oil is gasified on the spot by injecting steam, and siphoned off. An energy audit of the process would record: there are about 90 liters of oil contained in one ton of tar sand, and to extract and process it to a form comparable to crude oil requires an amount of energy equivalent to the yield from approx. 20 liters of oil. The energy bottom line is therefore that about 70 liters of oil can be obtained from every ton of tar sand.

The process consumes large areas, comparable to strip mining for metal ores or coal. The rising world market prices for crude oil in recent years are the reason why the extraction of oil from oil sand and shale, which was initially conducted on a small scale, has expanded. Today's manufacturing costs are estimated at about $40 per barrel, which is approximately 2.5 times higher than present oil production costs from the fields in the OPEC countries.

2.3 Natural Gas

Natural gas deposits, like oil deposits, can be accessed both onshore and offshore. Large deposit areas exist in Siberia and in the North Sea, off Norway, to cite one example from each of these recovery methods. Natural gas is extracted from the same depths as petroleum. The pressure in the deposit area is sufficient to drive the natural gas to the surface. Due to its geological origin, the raw gas is of varying quality, and not in a chemical form that would permit it to be immediately passed on to the consumer; for example, it contains heavy-metal components. Another distinction is between so-called sour, or acidic, gas and so-called sweet gas, with the sweet gas deposits predominating. The terms sweet and sour refer to the content of hydrogen sulfide (H_2S) in the gas: if it is greater than 1%, the gas is considered "sour gas," at less than five parts per million (ppm), it is called "sweet gas," and if it falls in the range in between, it is called "lean gas."

The processing of the natural gas begins at the drill hole. Depending on the quality and type of the gas, sand must be removed, the gas dried by adding glycol or methanol to limit the danger of corrosion, and larger, liquid hydrocarbons, i.e., those with particularly long-chained or large-ring molecules, must be condensed. Then, in the processing plant, hydrogen sulfide is precipitated off if necessary, and, after a chemical transformation process, shipped to the chemical industry in the form of sulfur. The carbon dioxide contained in the natural gas must also be removed by low-temperature processing, and then the nitrogen, too, is removed. After this processing and the addition of odors for safety, the natural gas then leaves the plant, headed for the consumer. Pipelines a meter in diameter carry it at a pressure of approx. 80 bar to the cities or to the bulk purchasers, such as large chemical plants. To maintain the pressure, a compressor station is installed approximately every 80 to 100 km. This is normally carried out with turbine-operated compressors, which are themselves powered by energy from natural gas withdrawn from the pipeline. Thus, 15% of the natural gas from Siberia must be earmarked for its own transportation to the consumption centers in Central Europe. The gas is then distributed via the local networks in the streets of the cities at a pressure of about 3 bar, which, for safety reasons, is then reduced to a few millibars of pressure at the household service connection; finally, it is burned in the boiler or kitchen stove.

Drilling for petroleum and natural gas is very expensive, therefore the drill holes must be exploited to the maximum, i.e. full-throttle, all year around. The same also applies to the expensive natural gas pipelines. Natural gas consumption is different in the summer and winter, however, so that additional storage depots are maintained to permit a more even import level. The capacity of the more than forty depots in operation in Germany, for example, equals about 20% of the country's annual gas consumption. They are designed as pore storage in rock, or as hollowed-out cavities in salt deposits; this is called cavern storage. After a severe winter, they are usually virtually empty.

2.4 Nuclear Fuels

The only fissionable nuclear fuel which occurs in nature is the uranium isotope U-235. It is present in natural uranium with a share of 0.7%. However, fissionable material can also be produced in nuclear reactors from thorium 232 by transforming it into artificial uranium 233, and from the normally non-fissionable uranium isotope U-238, by transforming it into plutonium 239 and higher isotopes. The latter occurs automatically during the operation of nuclear reactors, so that after a certain operating time, some of the electric power is produced by splitting the plutonium built up within the nuclear power station. Uranium is a trace element, i.e., it is present in very small quantities almost everywhere in the soil. This is also the reason for the natural "background radiation" on earth, since uranium and the products of fission created by its radioactive decay are very common. For example, problems with radon, a naturally occurring inert gas which escapes from certain building materials, and can be dangerous to human health if allowed to concentrate excessively due to improper ventilation, are well known.

The uranium deposits which occur in nature have uranium concentrations of about 2%. Uranium with this high concentration is particularly mined in the Canadian province of Saskatchewan. The uranium is found several hundred meters beneath the earth's surface, and is brought out with large vehicles moving through tunnels leading deep into the earth. The final product of this process is a uranium oxide compound (U_3O_8) called yellow cake, after its yellow color. It is the raw material used to make uranium hexafluoride, which is fed in a gaseous state to the enrichment plant. Here, a very complex technical process ensures that the isotope ratio remains shifted. At the end, the uranium contains a 3–5 % concentration of the isotope U-235, and is therefore well suited for use in nuclear power stations. There, it is filled into fuel rods in tablet form, as uranium dioxide.

In other uranium deposits, in which the uranium is not, as in Canada, very highly concentrated locally, it is often mined together with a large number of other metals and trace elements in vast strip mines. Because of the low concentrations, huge quantities of earth must be moved, and large areas consumed. However, this is not done specifically for the uranium. The mining of copper, which is so widely used in everyday life, is also carried out in large open pits, since copper occurs only in very low concentrations of less than 1%.

A nuclear power station requires about twenty-five tons of new uranium in an operating year. Compared with the amount of material needed for the production of the same quantity of electricity from fossil energy sources, twenty-five tons is not very much. To produce the same amount of electricity from hard coal, 2.5 million tons of hard coal would be needed. Ultimately however, these twenty-five tons of uranium must be considered in connection with the 15,000 to 35,000 tons of ore, i.e., soil, which must be moved in the mining process, because of the low concentration. But even this quantity is small, compared with the 2.5 million tons of hard coal. Internationally, there has been little forced resettlement of people due to uranium mining, since it generally occurs in sparsely populated areas.

2.5 Renewable Energies

Energy sources occurring in nature which, when viewed in a human time frame, are exhausted either not at all or only to a limited degree, are known as *renewable energies*. They include such sources as solar, wind, hydroelectric and geothermal energy. Figure 2 contains a summary of the possible uses of renewable energies.

Renewable energies have three different physical causes:

– First is the decay of natural radioactive isotopes, which generates heat (see uranium). Moreover, heat is conducted from the hot and liquid interior of the earth to the earth's surface. Nature has thus actually installed an underfloor central heating system for us. Unfortunately, its energy density is so low that we cannot, for instance, run around without shoes in winter, and that the snow is not melted by this "heater." Only a few milliwatts of energy per square meter reach the earth's surface.

– Only at those spots on the earth where anomalies have formed is the earth's heat, or *geothermal energy*, technically utilizable. Hot water deposits exist at certain spots on the earth, but they are a finite resource. At other spots, particularly those of volcanic origin, there are hot rock layers so near to the surface that they can be drilled into from the surface. If no such anomalies are utilizable, all that is left is the normal temperature gradient of "only" about 30°C of temperature difference per 1000 meters of depth (approx. one degree Fahrenheit per 100 feet). This means that at 4000 meters' depth, a temperature of about 120°C pertains. Today, techniques have been developed to make commercial use of heat at this temperature and from

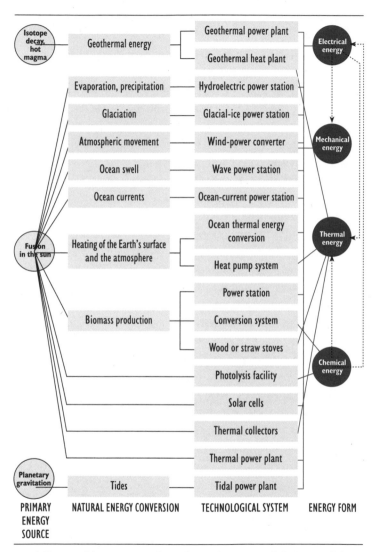

PRIMARY ENERGY SOURCE   NATURAL ENERGY CONVERSION   TECHNOLOGICAL SYSTEM   ENERGY FORM

Figure 2 Renewable energies: Their physical origin and their possibilities for conversion and use

this depth in the future, using the so-called "hot dry rock process."

– Geothermal power generation and geothermal heat production are state-of-the-art in those areas where these geological anomalies exist. Iceland, for example, obtains half of its energy consumption from geothermal sources. In many cases, however, geothermal energy use is not commercially feasible, compared with today's energy supplies based on oil and natural gas.

– The second physical source of renewable energy is the nuclear fusion in the sun, which is the reason why it sends radiant energy to the earth. We can use it directly, in the form of solar thermal systems to heat water, but nature also uses it for biomass production, for example for wood growth and plant growth generally. Different degrees of solar heating of the earth's surface produce ocean currents and atmospheric movements which we call wind energy. The evaporation and precipitation of water are also caused by solar radiation, and have been used to provide water power since ancient times.

– The third physical source of renewable energy is planetary gravitation. Masses attract one another. The mutual attraction of the earth and moon gives rise to the tides. For many years, attempts have been made to utilize tidal energy. To date, however, this has not proven commercially viable, with the exception of two major power stations, one in France and the other in Canada.

One characteristic of renewable energies – with the exception of hydroelectric power and geothermal energy – is that they are not permanently available. In particular, solar and wind energy provide a fluctuating, in some cases stochastically available, energy supply. When and how energy will be available is not very accurately predictable. Even if the long-term mean average values are well known, it is nevertheless hard to tie fluctuating energy sources into existing energy systems without some kind of storage system. We don't only want to take showers when the sun has just heated up the water, we want to take them when we need them. We also don't only need electricity when the wind is blowing, we want enough of it all the time, both in terms of quantity and of output. As long as the use of renewable energies remains additive to that of fossil energy sources, it can be assimilated well enough into existing energy systems, because it is generated in relatively small quantities. If, however, it were to account for a greater share of the energy mix, the questions of storage and adaptability to existing energy systems under the rapidly variable conditions of renewable energies would become increasingly urgent, both technically and economically.

The utilization of renewable energies is capital-intensive, and thus ultimately expensive for the consumer. The physical reason for that is the low energy densities with which nature provides it to us. In Central Europe, for example, solar irradiation provides as much energy per square meter over the course of a year as is contained in 100 liters of petroleum. Unfortunately, this energy is not provided in a thermodynamically high-quality form, as in the case of the petroleum, but rather in the form of radiation which, while it provides usable heat, provides it at a fairly low temperature. Heat can be stored from summer to winter only at a very great effort; the existing technologies for this are very inadequate. Systems for the transformation and use of renewable energies must be designed for great energy efficiency, at least in those countries where solar and wind energy are not present in abundance. Things are different for solar energy in sunnier countries. For a start, they receive twice as much solar energy as Central Europe; moreover, the intensity of the radiation is sufficient to heat up water for taking a shower using technically simple means.

Overall, the question as to the possibilities for the use of renewable energies is very complex. It depends, first, on the renewable energy source in question; second, on the technology used; and finally, on the supply, which differs widely worldwide. For this reason, the use of the renewable energies is the subject of an entire section of this book.

Energy Consumption and Population Growth

3 Statistics on Today's Energy Consumption

In this section, energy consumption will be described, using Germany as an example.

Primary energy consumption in West Germany increased continuously from 1950 up to the time of the first oil-price crisis in 1973. As a result of the leveling off of the economic boom, primary energy consumption then dropped for a few years, only to rise again after 1979. Because of the second oil-price crisis and the considerable price increase in energy for all consumer groups associated with it, the measures taken for energy savings and for more efficient energy use caused primary energy consumption to stagnate at just under 12,000 petajoules (PJ), or approx. 270 million TOE. The reunification of Germany initially caused energy consumption to increase statistically to approx. 15,000 PJ, or 350 million TOE, in 1990. Because of the restructuring of the economy in the new East German states, primary energy consumption was then reduced slightly, and amounted to approx. 14,000 PJ in 2007.

Germany, with 1.3% of the world's population, accounts for almost 3.5% of the world's primary energy consumption. Fig. 3 shows the share of each energy source in the country's energy consumption picture: as in all industrial nations, oil is the most important energy source. Coal – both hard coal and brown coal – natural gas and nuclear energy follow in importance. Renewable energies have a share of only a little over 1% of primary energy

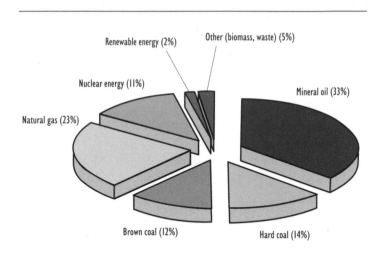

Renewable energy (2%)   Other (biomass, waste) (5%)

Nuclear energy (11%)

Mineral oil (33%)

Natural gas (23%)

Brown coal (12%)   Hard coal (14%)

Figure 3 Breakdown of primary energy consumption in Germany in 2007, by energy source

provision to date. Oil is used in the transportation sector and for heating plants. Hard coal is delivered as coke to the iron and steel industry, and is also used for electric-power generation in power stations, along with brown coal and nuclear energy. Natural gas dominates the heating market for buildings and for process-heat production in industry. An increasing amount is also used for electric-power generation.

This mix of primary energy consumption has developed over five different periods since 1950. During the 1950s, the energy supply was largely provided by hard coal. During the early 1960s, the expansion of auto traffic and the increased installation of oil-fired central heating systems caused a shift in the energy-supply pattern toward oil, which accounted for almost 55% of primary energy consumption by 1973. During the 1970s, the share of natural gas then increased substantially, partially thanks to the "shift out of oil" policy sparked by the 1973 oil crisis. During the 1980s, nuclear power expanded. The rise in the share of renewables and the established phase-out of nuclear power is the current phase – which is still continuing.

What the consumer uses is *end-use energy*, that is, the primary energy sources after processing. The statistics normally distinguish four consumer groups:

- *households* used 29% of end-use energy in 2006
- the *transportation* sector used 28%
- *industry* used 28%, and
- the *commercial sector*, e.g. the trades, sales and services, accounted for 15%.

The originally very different consumption structures for end-use energy in the East German and West German states have now largely been equalized, except for a higher share of district heat in the eastern states.

A comparison of figures for primary energy consumption and total end-use-energy consumption shows that statistically, only about two thirds of the primary energy used is accounted for as end-use-energy consumption. One major reason for that is the physically inevitable major energy loss involved in the production of electric power. The energy flow for Germany (Fig. 4) shows this in detail. Besides the losses in electric-power generation mentioned, energy is also needed for the energy-conversion process, e.g. for heating refineries and for transportation (e.g. electric power). Some secondary energy sources are used to make various products, such as synthetic materials, in the chemical industry, i.e., they are used in so-called non-energy-related

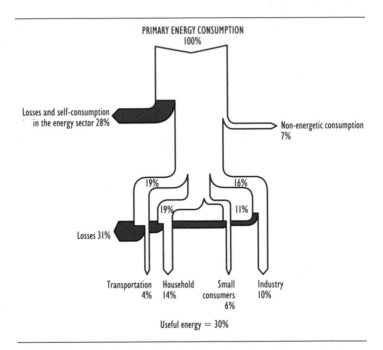

Figure 4 The energy flow picture for Germany: Breakdown of primary energy consumption into distributed and useful energy, by consumer group

consumption. The consumer turns only half of all end-use energy into useful energy, like light, heating, automobile propulsion, etc. The bottom line is that about one third of all primary energy is currently converted into useful energy. This apparently low share is actually high compared with other countries. Due to the laws of physics and the state of the art, no better degrees of effectiveness are possible to date.

In Chapter 14, on energy efficiency, a number of possibilities are introduced to increase the conversion rate. Moreover,

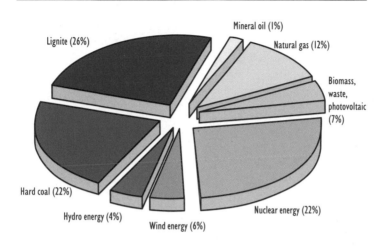

Figure 5 Percentage breakdown of electric-power generation in Germany in 2007, by primary energy source used

that there are still great potentials for the reduction of energy consumption, with no loss in comfort, e.g. by better insulation of buildings.

Germany is not independent of events on the world energy market with regard to its energy supply. Its only significant deposits of primary energy sources are hard coal and brown coal, and gas reserves that can no longer be expanded. The hydroelectric-power potential has largely been exhausted. For the security of its energy supply, Germany is therefore dependent on energy imports, particularly on the hydrocarbons petroleum and natural gas, as well as on uranium. For reasons of cost, increasing quantities of hard coal are imported, even though Germany has some deposits of its own.

About a third of all German primary energy consumption is used for the generation of electric power, as shown in Fig. 5, by the primary energy sources used. In 2007, total electric-power generation amounted to 630 terawatt-hours (TWh), so that on average, 7700 kWh of electric power per year are produced per capita in Germany, half of it from coal. Another quarter is provided by nuclear energy. The use of natural gas in power stations is a little more than 12%, and increasing. At present, hydroelectric power, wind energy and other renewable energies contribute 13% to the electric-power mix – and they are on the rise.

The figures for electric-power generation are gross values, i.e., they include all electricity produced. A minimal part of that is used by the power stations themselves, for their own needs. Total electric-power generation is included, i.e., both the production of industrial enterprises for their own use, and that of power stations, for supplying the general public.

3.1 Energy Use Worldwide

Worldwide primary energy consumption has risen considerably since 1950. After the oil price rises of the 1970s, it dropped slightly for several years. Since 1984 however, a considerable continuous increase in world energy consumption has once again been evident, boosted in particular by growing demand in Asia, which amounted to a 17% rise just between 2000 and 2006. In absolute terms, this means that statistically speaking, worldwide demand grew by an amount equal to half of Germany's annual energy consumption *every year* during this period. The fossil energy sources petroleum, hard coal and natural gas together cover more than 80% of worldwide primary energy consumption. Figure 6 shows the details.

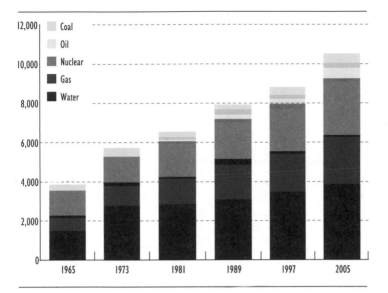

Figure 6 The development of world primary energy consumption, million TOE

For the sake of completeness, we should note what world electric-power production is, by comparison with Germany's. It amounts to 19,000 TWh, or approximately thirty times Germany's production. Worldwide coal accounts for about 40% of electric-power generation; gas provides 19%, and hydroelectric power 16%, the same as the worldwide share of nuclear energy. Oil accounts for 7%, and renewables – apart from water – for 2%. To put the worldwide figures for electric-power generation into perspective, another comparative figure is useful: if people in all countries used as much electricity as do those in Germany, worldwide electric-power generation would almost triple.

4 Energy Consumption in Everyday Life

When the gas or electric bill arrives in the mail is when you realize that you, too, are an energy consumer. If it makes you stop and think, you may assign your energy consumption to one of three different categories:

— direct energy consumption in the form of natural gas or fuel oil, electric power, and gasoline or diesel from the gas station
— energy consumption which you activate by using public transportation, for example if you take a train, bus or airplane to go on vacation; its price is a component of the cost of your ticket
— and third, the energy needed to produce the things we buy to meet your daily needs, such as food, clothing and home appliances.

We may still have a sense of the size of our energy consumption in the first category. For the second and third groups, however, we generally lack any concept of the level of our consumption, since it is not directly obvious to us. Therefore, let us take a look at the following examples, to see how high our actual energy consumption really is. Obviously, the circumstances in which people live are very different, as are their behavior and how they deal with energy, so this example will not exactly fit everyone's situation.

4.1 Example: A Four-Person Household in Germany

Let us take a look at a family of four, and start with their heating consumption. That depends on how big their living space in their apartment or house is, what its thermo-technical condition is, and how they handle ventilation. If it is an older detached home, built during the 1980s for example, the average heating energy use will come to about 15 liters of fuel oil or a comparable 15 cu. m. of natural gas per square meter of living space per year. If it is an apartment house of the same insulation standard, the heat consumption will be around 15% lower, as a result of the more compact ratio between the external surface and the living space. If the building has a good insulation standard, for example if it was built at the end of the 1990s, the energy requirement for heating will drop to 60% of the values mentioned above. Heating energy is needed to have warm rooms. These stay warm as long as their energy losses are compensated for from the heat from the radiator. These losses are the result of heat dissipation through the walls and windows, and from the exchange of air. Repeated opening of windows a crack causes considerably greater energy loss than opening the window completely for a short, quick air exchange. The better the structural state of the walls and the windows, the more important the effect of letting some air in correctly.

Given 100 sq. m. of living space, assuming a medium insulation standard, and taking into consideration the energy losses at the boiler, about 1200 liters of fuel oil or cubic meters of natural gas would be needed for heating. Assuming that four persons live in the apartment, 300 liters of fuel oil are consumed per capita annually. Add to that the energy consumed heating water for showers and baths, which depends primarily on the water quantity consumed ("standard requirement:" 30 liters per person per day). Empirical values show that a hot-water heating system in a four-person household will use another 300 liters of fuel oil. That boosts the per capita consumption of our household to about 375 liters of fuel oil or 375 cubic meters of gas per year. In many apartment houses, the warm water is heated by electricity for billing purposes, which means that the residents use about 650 kWh of electricity per capita. For heat consumption too, actual figures in individual cases may differ considerably from these approximate figures.

Additional household electric-power demand is dependent on the appliances and the apartment size. For statistical purposes, there are several different types of household. In Germany for example, a four-person household consumes about 4000 kWh per year, or 1000 kWh per capita, on average.

The first of the three groups of energy use mentioned at the outset also includes the purchase of energy at the gas station. The average fuel consumption of a car in Germany in 2002, according to a road-performance survey supplemented by data from test consumption, was 8.1 liters per 100 km, or 29 mpg. It has been improving slightly in recent years, due to the increasing share of diesel vehicles in the fleet. The statistical value for the annual road performance of privately used cars was 12,000 km, and for vehicles used for business, 21,000 km; for all cars, the average was 13,400 km in that year. We will use the last figure here. That yields a total for our family of 1080 liters of fuel use a year, or 270 liters per capita. Here, we should actually take into account that, statistically, Germany has one car for every two inhabitants. Our household should therefore have two, and hence twice the above road performance. However, let us assume that this is not the case, and that instead, our family makes use of public transportation, as described below.

In addition to the direct energy uses discussed above, let us now add those our family causes by using public transportation. If you board a streetcar or a train, you start to uses an entire chain of energy supply which, economically speaking, you pay for with your ticket. The energy consumption of public transportation per passenger depends very much on whether the streetcar or commuter train is running almost empty in the evening, or is jam-packed in rush hour. Here, investigations have shown that we can assume an all-day average energy consumption per person of about 3.8 liters per 100 km for commuter trains, and 1.7 liters per 100 km for streetcars (gasoline/diesel equivalent). Average consumption on city bus lines is somewhere in between. The streetcar itself is very energy-efficient, but it must be taken into account that the production of electricity involves major physically transformation losses at the power station, where two and a half times as much energy is expended as is used in the vehicle. If one uses public transportation for a short-distance commute and in addition for an occasional shopping trip, one will easily accumulate 2000 km per year of travel by this means. That increases the list of energy uses per capita by our family by an additional fifty-five liters of oil equivalent per year, assuming a mix of means of transportation. But vacation time is drawing near, a flight to a well-deserved vacation location is planned. That resort is 3000 km away from home, which means 6000 kilometers of air travel in a completely full vacation airplane, round trip. The airline companies calculate per capita energy consumption on the order of magnitude of 3.5 liters of kerosene per 100 km of flight.

It is now time for an initial interim audit of our family's energy consumption. All energy uses refer to primary energy use and have been converted to kilowatt hours, which is used here as a physical energy unit, so that the energy involved in not necessarily electric power. When reconverting these amounts to primary energy, losses at the power station (degree of effectiveness: 40%) and in the refinery (degree of effectiveness: 95%) must be taken into account. The interim balance sheet per capita per year for our family is then as follows:

- For heating: 300 liters of oil, with losses at the refinery × 1.05

  equivalent to 3150 kWh
- For heating water: 75 liters of oil under consideration of the losses in the refinery × 1.05

  equivalent to 790 kWh
- For the electric-power consumption: 1000 kWh, with losses at the power station × 2.5

  equals 2500 kWh
- For driving a car: 270 liters of fuel, with losses at the refinery × 1.05

  equivalent to 2835 kWh
- For using public transportation: 55 liters of oil equivalent,

  equivalent to 550 kWh
- For flying: 210 liters of kerosene, with losses at the refinery × 1.05

  equivalent to 2205 kWh

  Total: 12,030 kWh.

This amount of energy consumed so far represents the energy contents of almost 1.5 tons of hard coal or 1500 liters of crude oil per year. A look at the assumptions does not reveal a life-style based on particularly profligate energy use, in terms of our normal life. By contrast, imagine an energy audit of a manager whose job requires him to visit production centers on different continents once a month.

In addition to this energy budget, we must also consider the energy used in the third category, that is, what must be expended to produce the products we need for our daily lives, and which we buy as household goods and appliances. The exact calculation of the expenditure of energy connected with the production of such appliances is very detailed. However, simplified estimates can be carried out based on the monetary value of the goods. The production and sales values of an economic sector are known from official statistics. The statistics of the energy industry also record the consumption of various types of energy by sector of the economy. Recalculating the energy sources back to primary energy yields the specific energy consumption figures per €100 for products of a given sector of the economy. In Germany for example, the Federal Statistical Office ascertains what households spend their money on. Using these figures, we can obtain the following rough breakdown of the use of the net income of our four-person household, where net income means income minus taxes and social insurance payments. In 2005 for example, it amounted to €2770 per month as a national average. This income was used as follows:

— for rent, exclusive of heating   19%
— for the general cost of living: food, health,
  newspapers, repairs   29%
— for interest, insurance and other financial services: 11%
— for such purchases as clothing, furniture, cars etc.   25%
— for recreation, vacation, travel, etc.   9%
— for energy, including electric power, fuel oil, gas,
  hot-water   7%

Following the statistics over time, we discover that the share of energy in the budget of households is on the increase.

Assigning household expenses to business sectors and taking

their energy consumption into account, monthly household expenses cause an additional primary energy consumption of 1940 kWh per month. For our four-person household, that means another 5800 kWh of energy consumption per year.

Altogether, we can see that the annual per capita energy consumption of our family thus adds up to 17,830 kWh, which represents the energy contents of 2.2 tons of hard coal or 1800 liters of oil per year. Statistically speaking, therefore, the energy contents of a large tanker truck would just suffice to provide energy for three four-person households for a year. However, if we want to be scientifically precise, our energy balance will not end even here. For we also all take advantage of infrastructural services of the government, such as the use of public buildings, freeways and hospitals. These, too, need energy to be built and operated, energy which is not yet accounted for in the above audit.

4.2 Comparison with India

How would this energy audit for a four-person household change, if we were to apply it in India? There, the differences between the standards of living and of levels of energy consumption between various groups of the population are much greater than in Central Europe; indeed, millions of people there still have no access at all to commercial energy. The audit would therefore depend very largely on which household we were to choose for the purposes of our comparison. So let us perhaps imagine our four-person household as a family living in one of India's medium-sized cities. The father is a department head in a company, and has an academic education; he thus belongs to India's middle class. Such a living situation would be reflected by the following energy consumption pattern:

- During the three winter months, about 170 kWh of electricity would be needed per month. About 25 to 30 kWh of that would be used for light, and 60 to 70 kWh for hot water and heating with a fan heater. The rest would be used by the other electrical appliances.
- Air conditioning would be necessary during the summer months, driving electric-power consumption up to approx. 200 kWh per month, of which 100 to 125 kWh would be needed for the AC unit alone. We are assuming that the husband and wife both work, and that the air conditioner would normally not be used during the day, except on holidays. In case of non-energy-conscious users, this figure could climb to 300 kWh per month.
- Our family cooks with gas from gas cylinders, which are exchanged when they are empty. About 10 kg of liquefied gas are needed per month. In addition, the use of microwave ovens is also on the increase.
- The road performance of a small car comes up to 9000 km per year, which burns about 600 liters of fuel.

As in the case of the German household, we will now convert these values to primary energy use. With an additional allowance for public transportation, we then arrive at an energy consumption level of 3900 kWh per year, or about 30% of the German consumption level.

Now let us take a closer look at these differences. Electricity can be in short supply in India, at least at certain times of the day. Moreover, in terms of the purchase power of consumers, it is expensive. Therefore, our Indian family does not, unlike their German counterpart, heat or cool several rooms to the desired temperature, but only one room, and only when the family is in it. Also, in India, it is possible, weather permitting, to heat water with simple solar systems, which gives our family here an energy advantage over the German family. Short-distance public transportation, mostly buses, are also more fully occupied than in Germany, which cuts the per-capita amount charged to our family for this item. On the other hand, most vehicles are older, and thus have higher fuel consumption. We are assuming no vacation trips.

In conclusion, let us compare the electric-power needs of our two households. Indian households generally lack tumble-driers and dishwashers, and have many fewer lighting appliances. The standard lighting of a living room is provided by a fluorescent tube and in some cases also by a light bulb. This combination, which may sound surprising at first, is due to the unreliable local electric-power supply system. The power grids and power-station capacities are not always able to meet the demand for power. This frequently leads to major drops in voltage. For physical reasons, fluorescents lights then turn themselves off, while light bulbs "only" go dim. Nowadays CFLs capable of operating at low voltages are becoming popular. We are here leaving aside the question as to the losses or gains in living comfort provided by higher or lower energy-consumption levels.

Due to its lower income level, our Indian household simply buys fewer goods than our German family, so that the energy requirement for the production of these goods is also lower than in Germany.

The purpose of the above comparison has been to show what energy is used for in everyday life. The comparisons may also be food for thought about how a reduction of our everyday energy needs may be possible.

5 The Poor and the Rich

Geographically speaking, energy consumption is distributed unevenly around the world. This is due not only to different population densities, but also to the difference between rich and poor, as well as to the difference between greater and lesser efficiency in managing energy. Table 2 shows some demographic data and the specific primary energy use per capita of the population of selected countries and of the world. Two inequalities can be seen immediately: first, the differences among the industrialized countries; and second, the differences between the industrial and the developing countries.

The reasons for the different per capita primary energy consumption among the industrialized countries have to do with their climatic conditions, their population densities, the consciousness prevailing in their populations about energy, and of course their industrial structure. Comparing the USA with Germany, for instance, it is apparent that American per capita energy consumption is approximately twice as high as the German level. One reason has to do with climate: buildings in the USA must be air-conditioned in the summer; in Germany, virtually no homes have air conditioning. One might object that, at least in the southern half of the US, there is generally less need for energy for heating in winter, or even no need at all in some areas, which is true. However, it must then be considered that it takes almost twice the specific energy to air-condition a room as to heat it, if the humidity is high. The large distances in America are another reason for the higher energy consumption in that country. To transport a person on a long-distance flight in a well occupied airplane takes almost four liters of kerosene per 100 km per person. In the area of transportation, energy consumption in large countries is therefore greater than for example in Central European countries, which are smaller and relatively densely populated. Here, we must add, however, that in the USA, energy savings in the range of travel of several hundred kilometers would definitely be possible if rail transportation were used; however, the railroad system is very poorly developed. Moreover, lower taxes in the USA make energy prices much lower than in Europe, which leads to a lower level of awareness of the need to save energy.

Region	Population in millions	Primary energy consumption per capita in TOE	Electric-power consumption per capita in kWh
World	6,430	1.8	2,600
USA	297	7.9	13,600
Germany	82	4.2	7,100
Japan	128	4.2	8,200
Poland	38	2.4	3,400
China	1,310	1.3	1,800
Brazil	186	1.1	2,000
India	1,094	0.5	480
Ethiopia	71	0.3	40

Table 2 The populations and per capita primary energy and electric-power consumption levels, worldwide and in selected countries, 2005

An amusing example of the effect of different industrial

structures on energy consumption in industrialized countries is shown by the example of Germany and Luxemburg. Statistically speaking, the average Luxemburger surprisingly enough consumes twice as much energy as the average German, and thus, in spite of Luxemburg's high population density and – extremely – short distances, about as much as the average American. How can this be? The reason is the industrial structure of the little country with its high-input steel industry, which drives the statistics up.

Ethiopia is one of the poorest countries of the world. With 64 million inhabitants, its population is about equal to that of Britain and Ireland combined. But those people consume only one twelfth of the energy per capita available to Germans. The discrepancy is even more drastic regarding the consumption of electric power. The average Ethiopian uses only 36 kWh per year – including his or her share of the power consumption for the production of goods, telecommunications, and such public utilities as schools, hospitals etc. The corresponding value for the electric-power consumption per capita in Germany is 7100 kWh per year. Note that this figure reflects consumption; the figure of 7700 kWh per capita (p. 36) mentioned above refers to production. The 10%-plus difference is accounted for by the self-consumption of the power stations, and losses in the grid.

Such emerging-market nations as China and India have seen a major increase in energy consumption in the recent years, although the per capita rise is masked in the case of India by a considerable population increase. For the sake of clarity, the following figures are not given in the official energy unit, joules, but rather in "tons of oil equivalent" (TOE), which, as we recall, is the amount of primary energy equal to that obtained from burning a ton of oil. In 1990, specific energy consumption in China was 1.1 TOE per year; it then increased to 1.2 TOE per capita in 2005. India consumed 0.4 TOE in primary energy per capita in 1990, which dropped to 0.35 per capita in 2005, because of the great increase in the population. These figures reflect both the surging growth of industrialization in these countries and the problems of increasing population. However, both countries still fall considerably short of the worldwide average value of 1.7 TOE per capita – to say nothing of the gap between them and the industrialized countries.

Not all energy is the same – not in terms of its manageability, of the complexity of the technical systems needed to produce, store and use it, or with regard to the availability of particular energy sources. Therefore, behind the per capita data on energy consumption lies a different mix of energy sources. While those industrialized countries like Germany or Japan which are in the medium range in the consumer statistics depend on a broad energy mix of energy sources ranging from coal and oil through natural gas and nuclear power to an increasing share of renewables, there are some energy sources which are entirely absent in the developing countries. These countries are not capable of using very capital-intensive, high-tech and high-investment energy sources. For this reason, their major sources are wood for basic rural energy requirements, and otherwise oil, not only for transportation, but also for electric-power generation. Natural gas, nuclear energy and technically more demanding forms of renewables, such as wind power, are lacking. However, such emerging-market nations as India, Brazil and China are going the way of the industrialized countries: they use all the energy sources that their technical and economic capabilities permit. Hence, for example, all three countries have both nuclear power and natural-gas supply systems. Countries with large areas and high specific energy requirements, such as the USA and Canada, are characterized by a very high energy demand in their transportation sectors. While they use all energy sources, oil is present in their energy mix to a greater than average proportion, because mobility is based on this energy source. Since mobility is a basic human need, guaranteeing this mobility is of much greater importance, to some extent psychologically, in these countries than in densely populated countries or metropolitan areas with transportation infrastructures based on electrically powered mass transportation. Americans therefore consider a guaranteed sufficient supply of oil for the transportation sector not only an important economic issue, but also view it from the point of view of protecting their personal freedom.

6 Does Energy Consumption Follow Population Growth?

The number of people on earth is growing continuously. In 1950, some 2.5 billion people lived here; by 1990, there were already 5.5 billion, by 2002, 6.2 billion, and in 2006 approx. 6.6 billion. According to UN estimates, there could be about 8.5 billion people on earth in 2025, or 2.3 billion people more than today. The birth rate is lower in the industrialized countries, however, and higher in the developing countries.

6.1 The Division into "Prosperity Classes"

In its report *Beyond Economic Growth*, published in 2004, the World Bank classified countries according to their gross national products (GNP) per capita, and grouped them into three categories, based on conditions in 1999:

1. Low-income countries, i.e. those with less than $760 per capita of GNP
2. Medium-income countries, i.e. those with between $760 and $9400 per capita of GNP, and
3. High-income countries, i.e. those with more than $9400 per capita of GNP.

For purposes of comparison and classification: the gross national product of Germany that year was about $30,000 per capita. Of the almost 6 billion people reflected in the statistics in 1999, 40% were in the first, or low-income group. The medium-income group accounted for 45% of the world's population, and the high-income group, 15%.

One interesting aspect is that average life expectancy of the people in low-income countries is sixty-three, or about 20% lower than that in high-income countries, where it is seventy-eight. Thus, statistically speaking, life expectancy obviously depends on the national income of a country, the gross national product. For this reason, an analysis of world population growth must, in addition to higher birth rates, also consider the factor of longer life expectancy as a result of an increased standard of living in the developing countries. Thus, if we could succeed in significantly increasing the standard of living in the developing countries, including in the emerging-market nations like China and India, 100 million people more people would be alive in 2025 than otherwise.

Basically, the birth rate is evidently determined by the standard of living and the social safeguarding systems existing in a country as a result of that standard. In the industrialized countries, it is therefore lower than in the developing nations. Realistically, it must be assumed that the standard of living in most developing countries will not, within the next twenty to twenty-five years, rise to a standard that would cause the birth rate to drop appreciably. According to these assumptions, a population increase of about 1.9 billion people by 2025, or 47% over the 2002 level, can be predicted for the developing countries. They would then account for 75% of the world's population.

The conclusion is that population increase does not significantly depend on increased life expectancy so much as it does on the birth rate. The total population of the developing countries, and of the world as a whole, is determined essentially by high birth rates in the developing nations.

A reduction of the population increase by such epidemics as AIDS has not been included in the considerations, but under today's conditions, it cannot be ruled out for all parts of the world.

6.2 Growth of Energy Consumption

If we transfer this three-way division of the world's population to the realm of energy consumption, and also modify the classification of countries to base it on their status on the path to industrialization, the figures shown in Table 3 emerge for 2002:

	Population in millions	Consumption in		Consumption per capita	
		EJ	Million TOE	GJ	TOE
Industrialized countries	1,200	226	5,390	188	4.5
Emerging-market countries	700	57	1,330	79	1.9
Developing countries	4,300	152	3,640	35	0.8
World	6,200	435	10,360	70	1.7

Table 3 Breakdown of worldwide primary-energy consumption in 2002, by groups of countries (information shown in two different energy units)

The table shows that the approximately 20% of the world's

people who live in the industrialized countries are responsible for 50% of the world's energy consumption. We therefore need to answer the question as to how energy consumption is to develop in the future, and what the relationship is between that consumption and the available reserves. To get a sense of the orders of magnitude, it could be helpful to image some simplified scenarios. We will pose three questions:

1. What energy consumption would result if the world's population of 6.2 billion people in 2002 were to rise to 8.5 billion people by 2025, and today's average worldwide per capita energy consumption were to remain unchanged?
2. How much of today's world energy reserves would still be left in 2025, and how long could these reserves then be expected to last? Let us also make the optimistic assumption that world reserves of fossil energy sources will double by 2025, to 73,000 EJ (1.74 trillion TOE). All additional people are to use as much energy, on average, as the people already living today.
3. On the other hand, how long would these energy resources last if worldwide per capita energy consumption were to increase to the standard of the industrialized countries by 2025?

The answers to these questions are as follows:

1. Initially, annual world energy consumption would increase from 440 EJ – or 10.5 billion TOE – in 2002 to 580 EJ, or 14 billion TOE. Assuming that the population increase proceeded linearly from 2002 to 2025, the total primary energy consumption during this time period would be 11,700 EJ, or 280 billion TOE.

2. That would leave 61,000 EJ, or 1.47 trillion TOE of available reserves in 2025, which could be expected to last for 104 years.

3. In this case, these reserves would only last another twenty-five years.

Let us now examine these questions and answers for their validity. Of course, they are theoretical, inasmuch as the question does not take into account the fact that growing worldwide energy demand is concentrated primarily on oil and gas, and not so much on coal. However, that fact makes these figures all the more ominous, for it means that the oil and gas reserves will last even less long than the energy reserves overall, since coal accounts for the major share of all reserves.

What is unrealistic in Scenario 3 is the idea that the standard of living of the entire world could be raised to the level of the industrialized countries within twenty-three years, and that the whole world would then have the average per capita energy consumption of these countries.

Thus, the questions and answers merely serve to convey a sense of the upper limits of energy demand. The trends are clear, however. They mean that worldwide energy needs are very likely to increase further very considerably. Since energy demand is predominantly concentrated on hydrocarbons, due to their importance for transportation and their good storage and shipping characteristics, the above assumptions as to how long reserves will last appear rather optimistic. One might of course argue that with higher energy prices, more hydrocarbons could be produced. The question would then be whether the developing countries in the lowest category would, with their low incomes, still be able to obtain more hydrocarbons – primarily oil – on the world market in order to attain the world average of per capita consumption. The increase in world energy consumption would then slow down.

6.3 Redistribution

Our considerations so far have not included any ideas for how to reduce world energy consumption by having industrialized countries handle energy more efficiently, that is, to cut their per capita energy consumption by energy savings or at least by improved utilization. In order to get an initial feeling for the order of magnitude of what is involved here, let us ask the following question:

Say that a country, in this case Germany, were to behave in an exemplary manner and managed to cut its primary energy consumption in half, based on today's level, i.e., every German resident would then consume only half as much energy, on average, as he or she does today. And let us say that the energy saved was to be shared out equally among the developing countries. How would things change for them?

Here is the answer: Germany would save 7500 PJ, or about 175 million TOE, of energy annually. If this were shared out equally among the people in the developing countries, their per capita energy consumption would only increase by about 5%. Clearly, one country alone cannot make a major dent in the problem.

We would also have to take into account the fact that cutting the energy consumption of an industrialized country in half while maintaining the same level of economic welfare would not be a short-term process. It would require several decades, since only by advances in energy-saving technologies and modification of consumer behavior could we achieve energy efficiency increases of such a magnitude. Realistically, therefore, no more than a 20%

saving should be assumed, and even this would require a large number of measures. After all, assuming that all industrialized countries were to save 20% of their primary energy consumption, and that these savings were to be used to benefit the developing countries, their per capita consumption could increase by 30%. That sounds like a lot, initially, and it is indeed a lot, relative to their present standard. But in absolute terms, their per capita energy use would then still only be a little over 1 TOE per year, while consumption in the industrialized countries would still be 3.6 TOE per capita, or 3.5 times as high. Nor would this absolute saving compensate for the increased consumption caused by the growth of the world's population through 2025; in other words, even assuming a 20% drop in consumption in the industrialized countries, worldwide energy consumption would still rise.

The above examples allow us to draw several cautious conclusions. Within the next two decades, the world's population will probably increase faster than its energy consumption. The reason is that the population increase is taking place in the developing countries, with lower per-capita incomes, and hence lower energy consumption. However, increasing demand for energy by the population means that in the long run, additional resources will have to be developed, and this can only be done with higher prices for energy. This will in turn dampen the growth of energy consumption, because the countries with low per-capita incomes and high rates of population increase lack the necessary foreign exchange to buy energy on the world markets. World energy consumption will increase in absolute terms, but that increase will lag behind world population growth. One contribution to alleviating this problem would be to increase energy efficiency and promote energy savings in the industrialized countries. If the target of a 20% saving in per-capita consumption could be realized within the next two decades, that would contribute to a slowdown in the increase in world energy consumption, and moreover ensure that cheaper energy resources would be available longer. The gap with the developing countries could be addressed in a more satisfactory manner.

Energy — A Commercial Product

7 Energy is a Commodity

The energy sources which occur in nature are traded, as are thousands of other goods that we use every day. The goal of the merchants is to meet the demand of their customers, and to obtain as much profit as possible in the process. Because of the significance of energy for the development of the economy and for general welfare, trade in energy is subject to special stipulations and conditions in some countries. There are only a few cases in which energy resources are not traded. The wood used to meet basic energy requirements in many rural areas in developing countries is for the most part gathered by family members, so it is not taken to market. Sometimes however, wood collectors gather it and sell it or trade it for other products; it too is then on the market. The use of renewable energy sources is often not traded, for example if solar thermal collector systems on a roof provide hot water to the home-owner. In the following, let us examine what the trade chain for energy sources looks like and which criteria determine the prices that consumers ultimately have to pay for energy. To do so, we will have to distinguish between the various energy sources.

7.1 Brown Coal

Brown coal has little market value. It suffers from the twin handi-
caps of low heating value and high water content, so that ship-
ment per unit of real energy content is expensive compared to
other energy sources, and trade is hampered. There is thus no
market for brown coal. In most cases, the mines belong to the
energy companies, and the coal is immediately burned in power
stations which also belong to those companies. The price level is
therefore not determined by the market through competition, but
is based on accounting costs within the respective corporation.

However, the minimal quantity of brown coal which is still
made into briquettes or coke and thus enters the heat-energy
market – in Germany, that amounts to only 7% of the brown coal
extracted – is of course subject to competition. The consumer
can buy coal from various dealers and compare the prices with
those of other energy sources, such as oil or natural gas, which
he or she could also use for heating. The pricing of brown coal
is not subject to any state regulation, since this energy source is
not marketed by a monopoly.

7.2 Hard Coal

Hard coal is different. Major coal deposits exist on all continents.
The main exporters of hard coal are Australia, Indonesia, China
and, of dwindling importance, South Africa and Russia. On the
other hand, Colombia and Venezuela are increasingly important.
In the exporting countries, a number of companies are involved,
and often are in competition with each other.

Important factors which affect the pricing of hard coal
are its ash content, its heating value and the share of volatile

components, which determines its combustion properties. The sulfur content is also an important factor with regard to local reduction of pollution. Different markets have been formed around the world. The power-coal market is primarily determined by the trade in coal qualities suitable for power stations. Another important worldwide market is the market for coke coal, which is needed for steel production. The criteria which determine the pricing are accordingly different. The following aspects are important from the point of view of demand: hard coal is subject to substitution competition on the electricity market, i.e., it is forced to compete against other energy sources with which electric power can also be produced. These include brown coal, natural gas and heavy fuel oil; in some countries nuclear power is also a competitor.

In the heat market, the customers are big industrial heat producers or industrial cogeneration systems, i.e., systems which provide both electricity and process heat needed for the production process. In the industrialized countries, hard coal has largely lost its household-heating market, for reasons of convenience. No one likes to drag coal upstairs from the cellar to the stove, or take out the ash every day. In developing countries such as China, however, hard coal is important as the energy source for households, including for cooking. That causes large-scale atmospheric pollution in China and other countries, since sulfur dioxide, carbon monoxide and other harmful gases are created when the coal is burned; they cause acid rain and winter smog. For this reason, the major cities are trying to move in the same direction as the industrialized countries have since the 1960s, and to replace coal as a home heating fuel by other energy sources, such as natural gas, which is easier to handle in terms of atmospheric pollution. In industry on the other hand, coal has largely kept its market position, both for reasons of cost and because factories have the possibility of building sulfur-scrubbing facilities. But here, too, coal has to compete against other energy sources, especially oil and natural gas.

Coke coal has a special role. It is a key element in the technical process of steel production, and cannot be replaced by any other energy source, since it not only provides energy, but also carbon atoms, which are chemically required in the process. The price of coke coal also rises or drops in response to changing demand, depending on the ups and downs of the steel industry. Due to the great economic growth in Asia in recent years and the resulting heavy demand for steel, bottlenecks have periodically developed on the coke-coal market, causing prices to double. Prior to that, however, there was a phase in which decisions were taken to shut down coking plants because no demand for coke coal was predicted over the long term.

The worldwide coal trade is primarily carried out between producers and consumers. Among the various types of contract, spot sales, i.e., short-notice price quantity agreements, have been gaining in importance. In the past, sales contracts valid for up to ten years were not uncommon; today, only quantity agreements are concluded for such periods; the prices rise or fall according to the demand for hard coal on various markets. For example, the import price of a ton of power-station coal, free German port border, fluctuated between €40 and €110 per ton during the period 2003 to 2008. The comparison with the hard coal which is mined under Central European terms is interesting: it costs up to twice as much.

7.3 Oil

Yet oil is the most interesting energy commodity. There is both an international raw oil market and an international market in refinery products. This market can be described as a partial monopoly on the supply side, because it includes only the OPEC cartel and a very few other suppliers, such as Russia. Oil prices are determined by several factors. The first is the price of crude oil itself, which is determined by supply and demand. Since the demand for oil has risen continuously in recent years, and new reserves have not been developed to the same extent, on the production side, the price of crude oil has been rising. Figure 7 shows the development of this price over the past two years.

We should note that while the prices have risen considerably, they are also subject to major fluctuations. They are far higher than the costs of extraction, which would be in the range of $6 to $20 per barrel for the bulk of the crude oil produced today. By contrast, world market prices for crude oil have surpassed $130 per barrel at the time of writing, almost double what it was when the German version of this book was written.

That very price tag indicates the second important factor affecting the pricing of crude oil: it is normally traded worldwide in US dollars. Thus, the exchange rates between national currencies and the American currency affect the local price of crude oil. The European Union has, since the launching of the euro, profited considerably from this, as the euro has risen against the dollar from the original 90 cents to over $1.50. The situation is very different for countries whose currencies have dropped in relation to the dollar, or have been devalued on the free market. For them, oil imports have become much more expensive. Developing countries have been particularly severely affected.

Until the 1970s, most shipments of crude oil were priced in

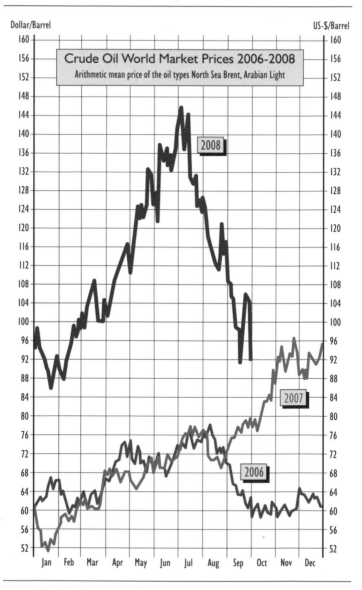

Figure 7 The development of oil prices on the market during 2006 through 2008 (Source: http://www.tecson.de/prohoel.htm)

longer-term contracts between refineries, oil corporations and producing countries. This changed with the politically motivated oil-price increases of 1973 and 1978. Previously, the smaller share of oil had been traded on the commodity exchanges, primarily the Rotterdam spot market; now, the tables were turned, and they have remained so. The trade in oil has now also become the object of speculation between financial funds. Particularly hedge funds, which aim at short-term profits even at the risks of great losses, like to participate in oil trading. It is hard to assess their exact effect on pricing, but occasional additional price increases of $3 to $5 per barrel, or 5% to 10% of the price of crude oil in 2006, are certainly possible. The advantages of commodity-market trading are obvious: in times when prices can rise and fall rapidly, market participants are reluctant to risk being bound by long-term contracts. Since large quantities of oil can only be transported internationally by tanker, it is possible to transport the oil exactly to those spots in the world where the best profits can be had.

7.4 The Role of OPEC

Under such conditions, it might occur to someone to create an artificial oil shortage, to push up prices. For example, oil tankers might sail around in circles for a while, and only reach their ports of call with considerable delay. Even if we cannot be sure that no such thing has ever been tried, it is not the usual method of doing business. Consumers who have repeatedly failed to be provided with oil in sufficient quantities will be on the lookout for alternative sources of energy, and be able to find them, in natural gas or coal, for example. Potentials for energy savings are available, too. The development to "move away from oil" has already happened once, at the beginning of the 1980s. In 1973, OPEC exported 1.5 billion tons of petroleum. Their average revenue from it, in the monetary value of the time, came to about $3* per barrel. In the short time span from then until the beginning of the 1980s, oil prices rose to over $33 per barrel (see Figure 8).

Initially, the oil customers, particularly the industrialized countries, could not react by reducing demand. They had no alternative technologies available, and a shift to other energy sources would take longer. They recognized, however, that they had to do something, and in a joint policy under the OECD for increased energy efficiency, decided on the one hand to improve the insulation of buildings, the efficiency of engines and the degree of effectiveness of boilers. On the other, Germany for example moved to replace oil with hard coal in electric-power generation, and many countries expanded their nuclear-power production. In order to bring in another conveniently shippable and storable energy source for the heat market in addition to oil, many industrialized countries supported the exploration for natural gas and the construction of capital-intensive natural-gas distribution systems. Exploration activities for oil in countries outside OPEC was boosted, and additional oil fields, such as those in the North Sea, which were now economically viable

---

* However, we must take into account that the dollar was considerably stronger at that time in relation to other currencies, and that the long-term currency depreciation, which has continued to this day, has of course had a considerable effect. Therefore, OPEC points out in its statistics that the crude oil price of $61 per barrel that pertained in 2006 was only about $12 per barrel in 1973 terms, when these effects are discounted. Roughly calculated, this means that a crude oil price of $130 per barrel has really increased "only" a little over tenfold since 1973.

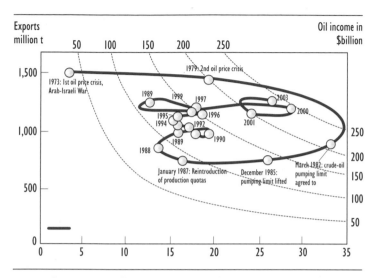

Figure 8 The progress of OPEC: Exports of oil and products, their price and the proceeds from them for OPEC, from 1973 to 2003

The value for 2005 is outside the diagram. At an export level approximately like that of 2001, OPEC received a sales volume of $430 billion at a mean oil price of $55 per barrel. Proceeds in 2007 probably exceeded $600 billion, since oil prices rose further, and there was a slight increase in export volume.

due to the higher prices, were tapped. As a result of these measures, the quantities of oil obtained from OPEC started to drop after about ten years. Under the laws of the market, prices then dropped again, too, and by 1987, OPEC was only able to sell less than half the quantity of oil it had sold in 1973. That caused a considerable change in revenues from oil exports for the OPEC countries. They had climbed from about $30 billion in 1973 to about $260 billion at the end of the 1970s, only to drop again to about $90 billion in 1988, due to the reduced sales volume and the reduced prices. Taking into account that these figures represent respectively current dollars, and have not been corrected for the effects of inflation, we can see how drastically this quantity-price game must have hit the economies of the OPEC countries.

OPEC has tried to counter the trend of dropping prices and the resulting reduced demand by means of agreements between its member countries to pump only a certain maximum quantity of oil for the world market. Unfortunately, these agreed-upon goals have not always been observed by all member countries. The reason has to do with the structure of OPEC. It was founded in 1960 with offices in Vienna, as a common-interest group of petroleum-exporting countries facing the large foreign oil corporations which extracted petroleum in their countries. Its members were Algeria, Ecuador, Gabon, Indonesia, Iran, Iraq, Kuwait, Libya, Nigeria, Qatar, Saudi Arabia, the United Arab Emirates and Venezuela. During the 1990s, Ecuador and Gabon withdrew. The membership structure shows that on the one hand, the Arab countries have generally low total populations and large oil deposits. They primarily needed oil exports as a source of income to permit them to lead the good life. Countries like Algeria, Ecuador, Gabon, Indonesia or Venezuela on the other hand have large populations which have to use their oil incomes to rapidly build up other economic sectors, so as, in the long run, to be able to create jobs and prosperity. Moreover, some countries, such as Indonesia, have limited oil reserves, so that they will not be able to depend on the income from oil over the long term. The interests of the latter group are thus considerably different from those of the first group. The latter group would like to sell as much oil as possible as rapidly as possible, to obtain high proceeds which will permit them to counteract the pressures of large and growing populations. All this has then led to price fluctuations – the opposite of the real purpose of OPEC. By accepting these price fluctuations, the export standard has been more or less maintained by OPEC over the past ten years. A new development has arisen since 2004, however. The unexpectedly high demand for oil from the high-growth emerging-market nations and the only moderate development of oil pumping capacities, along with the temporary loss of oil from particular countries like Iraq, has once again turned the world oil market into a seller's market. The prices of crude oil have increased again.

7.5 Oil as a Source of Tax Revenues

Now that a large number of effect factors which contribute to the pricing of oil have been discussed, the role of the state must also be examined more closely.

Since the Second World War, European countries have seen the sale of gasoline and diesel as an additional source of tax income in the transportation sector. Everyone knows that a major share of the price paid at the gas pump goes into the state coffers. For example, a liter of gasoline cost €1.45 in Germany in the spring of 2008 – about $8.80 per gallon. The price of crude oil was $100 per barrel at that time, which translated to about 43 eurocents per liter of crude oil at the going euro-dollar exchange rate. For the transportation of the crude oil and of the derivative products, the transformation of the crude oil into those products, gasoline or diesel, in the refineries, one could add about another 12 cents per liter. After granting the service-station owner 2 cents per liter, we can still see that about two thirds of the sales price is accounted for by taxes of one kind or another: the petroleum tax, the environmental tax and the value-added tax. It is up to the state to impose taxes wherever it considers it right, as long as it treats all citizens equally. The European concepts of high taxation of vehicle fuels have been historically determined by the situation in the 1950s and 1960s. Increasing motorization required rapid high investments in the development of a road network, money that was obtained by new tax revenues. Later, another factor become predominant – the desire to increase the energy efficiency of vehicles by artificially boosting the price of fuels. This seems to have worked quite well in the past. Fifteen years ago, a European quality medium-sized vehicle still consumed one third less fuel per kilometer than an American vehicle; in the US, gasoline was virtually untaxed. Now, the situation has evened out somewhat, since rising crude oil prices in recent years have almost tripled the cost of gasoline for consumers in the USA. While it is still less than half the European level, Americans are now choosing to buy thriftier new cars.

7.6 Oil from the Consumer's Point of View

Until now, we have primarily examined the commodity oil from the point of view of the suppliers. Let us now switch to the point of view of the consumer – the purchasing manager in a factory, or the private consumer who wants to refuel his or her car. Let us start with an analysis of the latter. At first glance, the fuel sector is a picture of direct competition between a large variety of service stations. You can fill up at a certain "brand," at a certain place, or wherever it suits you best. Ultimately however, only a few large corporations have divided Europe and the USA's service-station sector up between them, and even they have shown tendencies toward mergers recently. The game of supply and demand nevertheless operates here, albeit with smaller price differences. It is evident, for instance, that prices rise at gas stations along the routes of the streams of vacationer traffic. As the sunshine awakes in springtime, not only does the flow of traffic increase, so too does the price of gasoline at the pump on the weekends. At times, they also drop again, when demand falls, due to poor weather. All in all, a more or less autarchic demand behavior has been established here, however: there is little elasticity between price and road performance. Our decision to use our vehicle or not is not primarily made in view of the price of fuel, but due to other requirements or needs, such as job-related travel or simply the desire to get out into the countryside.

Technically speaking, oil as an energy source has great advantages. It is therefore the basis of individual transportation worldwide. More than 80% of worldwide mobility today is based on oil. It is simple to handle, even for ordinary people, and it has high energy density, so that a relatively small tank can take us a long way, as it proves a million-fold at the pump. Moreover, it is easy to transport and store. This has given oil a monopoly in the transportation sector.

From the point of view of the industrial purchaser, oil looks different. He needs it to heat his offices and his production plants, and particularly to produce necessary process heat, such as steam for sterilizing or boiling down, or for electric-power generation. The physical advantages of oil are very important to him, but other energy sources are available, too, for his purposes. In particular, oil competes here with natural gas, which has the same good physical and processing features, and also the advantage that it does not have to be stored locally. Thus, oil is in competition with other energy sources in the industrial sector. The same applies to its use in power stations. As a result of the "move away from oil" policy at the end of the 1970s, Germany for example made the decision not to use oil for electric-power generation, and gave preference to coal. This was different in other countries; oil still provides considerable electric-power generation in many countries, both developing and industrialized. Heavy fuel oil in particular is used here, as mentioned above in the description of the refining process.

7.7 Natural Gas

Natural gas competes with oil not only in the industrialized countries, but also increasingly in such emerging-market countries as China. Particularly for use in electric-power generation in power stations or for use in industrial enterprises, but also for heating buildings, natural gas has gained major market shares. In 1976, for example, only 16% of the apartment stock in Germany was heated by gas; by 2006, that had tripled to 48%. From the supply side, natural gas too is an oligopolistic structure. There is no grouping of countries comparable to OPEC in the oil industry, but nonetheless, natural gas is available in considerable quantities – in terms of worldwide demand – in only about fifteen countries. For the supply of Europe, the natural gas deposits in Russia, Norway, the Netherlands and the Mediterranean are particularly important. As a grid-bound energy source, the infrastructure for natural gas is very capital-intensive, as this figure illustrates: the existing natural gas pipelines from Siberia to Western Europe have lengths of up to 4500 km. The expenditures for building such pipelines, at today's new-construction prices, would range between €6 and €9 billion. The gas industry is therefore forced for economic reasons to exploit its investments, i.e. its extraction and transportation capacities, to the maximum, so as to be able to offer reasonable natural gas prices on the market. This favors the conclusion of longer-term sales contracts. This demonstrates a fundamental structurally difference from the oil industry. The transportation and storage of oil are technically less demanding than the transportation and storage of gas. These expenses are secondary in the oil industry; in the gas industry, they are the second most important cost factor after extraction.

In spite of these long-term sales contracts between gas producers and gas-pipeline corporations which transport the gas from Russia to Europe and bring it to the national markets, the prices are not necessarily fixed over the long term. Historically, there has been a pegging of the natural gas price to the oil price in some countries. If the price of crude oil rises or falls, the natural gas price follows along with it, with a time lag of a few months or so. This pricing policy has frequently been questioned politically. For example, it applies to the German market, but not to the British market. A comparison of the sales figures and prices in the two countries to date do not permit the conclusion to be drawn that natural gas would be cheaper for the consumer if its price were not pegged to oil. On the other hand, the reasons which led to this price-pegging twenty years ago, to prevent an excessive switch to cheap natural gas if oil prices rose, are no longer valid today.

These explanations show that primary energy is traded according to the laws of supply and demand on the world markets, and that oil is traded primarily on the spot market under short-term conditions. On the buyers' side, markets are being deregulated in ever more countries worldwide, i.e. energy sources are becoming aware of their mutual competition, but also of the competition between various suppliers. This is particularly true of the grid-bound energy sources, natural gas and electricity. We will therefore take a closer look at these two energy sources and their markets in the next chapter.

8 The Special Features of Grid-Bound Energy Sources

8.1 Deregulation Shapes the Markets

The high capital formation required for the grid-bound energy sources, natural gas, electricity and district heating, has in the past been the reason that most industrialized countries have not decontrolled their energy-supply markets. This simply meant that the supply areas were divided up between different utility providers. Competition was not permitted, so as not to bind still more capital, and thus cause higher prices for consumers. They could thus buy their gas and the electric power only from the utility provider responsible for the area in which they lived. These markets have been decontrolled in the USA and in Central Europe since the mid-1990s. The closed supply areas have been abolished, so that the different companies and newly established dealers can now offer their energy sources for sale wherever they see a demand. The buyer can shop around among the different companies; in some cases, natural gas has to be moved through the existing grid belonging to another company, for payment, of course. The central idea is that energy is a commodity like any other, and that pricing should be determined by market forces and not, as in the regulated market, by means of an accounting process with a profit surcharge.

The various cost structures of the grid-bound energy sources, natural gas, electricity and district heating, as compared with the non-grid-bound energy sources, oil and coal, are described below. Grid-bound energy sources have a high capital component, which makes it necessary for economic reasons to optimally exploit the available grids around-the-clock if possible. This, however, does not meet the needs of consumers who need different amounts of energy at different times of the day or year. This is the reason for example that district heating makes economic sense only where, in addition to housing, there are also such customers as laundries, hospitals or swimming pools, which need heat even in summer.

While the purchasers of hard coal or oil pay only for what they actually buy, i.e., the tons of hard coal delivered, or the liters of gasoline put into the tank, the consumers of the grid-bound energy sources must also pay so-called demand prices or base prices. This is a fixed price per month, which serves to cushion the high capital-bound expenditures of the provider. The consumer pays for the privilege of unrestricted access to the grid-bound energy supply. A similar cost structure to that of the grid-bound energy sources exists in telecommunications. Here too, major investments have been made in lines and air transmission rights, while the business expenses of the telecommunications network itself is fairly low. There is, however, a substantial difference between telecommunications networks and energy-supply networks. With energy supply networks, the line is never "busy," i.e., the consumer will not be cut off from service because only restricted capacities are available. He or she can expect to be able to tap any amount of energy at any time it is desired. If the telecommunications sector procedure were applied to grid-bound energy, the following would happen: when you stuck a plug into an electrical outlet or switched on your television set, a request would be sent via an information channel to the central load dispatching station, to inquire whether the necessary amount of energy and the power station capacity behind it were available now or not. The device would then either switch itself on or else a signal would light up showing "occupied," i.e. no energy delivery possible at present. This comparison shows the special demands to which our energy-supply system is subject.

District heat and electric power have two other characteristics which make them different from gas, and which affect trade and pricing. The first has to do with energy loss in transportation. District heat is a perishable commodity. Even with well insulated pipelines, the hot water loses heat, i.e., district heating cannot be transported and distributed over any distance desired. In large German cities, district-heat networks in practice span distances between the heat-production source and the consumer of perhaps 20 km, often less. In some countries, however, such as Siberia, with extreme climatic conditions, where district heating systems were formerly given political priority, considerably longer district-heat pipelines have been installed. In these cases, the temperature loss has to be compensated by introducing heat into the pipelines at the district-heat production site at much higher temperatures than the remote consumer will need. The – yet open – question then arises as to whether district heating is then still the best solution for energy supply.

Electricity also cannot be transported directly over long distances without considerable loss. Therefore, power stations tend to be built near to consumer centers, for economic reasons. Normally, electricity is transported as alternating current, because of its good transformability to different voltages, and because it is in that form when it comes out of the generator. According to the laws of physics, the higher the transmission voltage in the power lines, the smaller the losses will be. Therefore, the grid operators try to get the power from the power station to the vicinity of the consumers at as high a voltage as possible. The power grids are therefore built up at different voltage levels: in Germany for example, the voltage is boosted to 220,000 or 380,000 volts at the power station, transferred to major cities, and then transformed down to 110,000 volts, the level at which power is provided to the various neighborhoods of the city. There, it is in turn distributed to street-blocks at another lower voltage level of 30,000 volts, and finally brought down to the 230 or 400 volts with which people in Europe are familiar – in some counties, 115 V is standard – which we use at our electrical outlets and stoves. Large industrial consumers are frequently supplied directly at the high-voltage level, and take care of the distribution within their operations themselves.

A second special characteristic of electric power is that there is no storage system with enough capacity available. Although pump-storage plants exist, which pump water from the valley to basins at higher sites, letting it run back down and generate power when it is needed to meet peak demand, it is not economically feasible to build many pump-storage plants, and in some countries the topographical conditions do not permit it. Therefore, it is always necessary to produce exactly the quantity of electricity that the consumer demands. This consumer behavior is roughly known from an analysis of past behavior, but in practice, there are always deviations between the amount of power expected and the amount actually demanded. Therefore, power stations exist which can compensate for this difference by boosting or throttling their power output. That costs a lot of money, since these power stations ultimately produce little electricity, but their output must be available around-the-clock. The consumers pay for these costs through their electricity bills. And since sufficient storage is not possible, reserve power stations must of course also be kept ready. They are brought into operation if a facility has to be taken off line unexpectedly, for technical reasons. This too causes additional capital expenses. Thus, the electric-power industry, like the gas industry, is characterized by a cost structure with high amounts of bound capital in the grids and power stations.

8.2 Commodity-Exchange Trading

Electricity is a commodity. In decontrolled markets, certain amounts of the electricity produced are increasingly being traded on commodity exchanges. The gas industry is following in its footsteps. An important commodity exchange in Germany is the European Energy Exchange (EEX) in Leipzig. Trading at the exchange offers two advantages. First, the electricity producer would like to make fuller use of his power-station output, and can look for additional buyers at the exchange. Second, the buyer can try to buy cheap electricity, because he may run into a supplier who has not made full use of his capacities, and who wants to get at least a marginal return on his expenditures at a lower price. Like all trading, the trade in electric power takes place at the commodity exchange according to firmly predefined rules of the game. For example, there is something called *day-ahead trading*. One day in advance, the buyers announce the quantities of electricity that they are prepared to purchase at a given price, broken down by the hours of the day. The power producers in turn announce the quantities of electricity they would like to sell at which price, again, broken down by hours. They then try to find common ground. The results of the traded quantities and their prices are published, so that the commodity exchange participants can develop a good feeling for the quantity-price relationship. If no agreement is reached, the game starts over again.

8.3 Integrated Grid Systems

Europe is covered by interconnected high-tension grids. The reason is the connection of various energy sources: hydroelectric power from Austria can be delivered to the north, and in exchange, power from coal-fired plants in the north can be sent south. For example, because Italy has not kept up its construction of power stations sufficiently, large quantities of electric power are sent from France every day, with corresponding transmission-line losses. On the night in the summer of 2003 when a blackout struck Italy due to the faulty switch-off of high-tension lines in Switzerland, Italy had to import the entire output of four French nuclear power stations, about 5 GW. The deregulation of the electric-power market in the European Union has been the reason why large companies buy their electric power wherever it is the most favorable for them. Since then, the grids have been subjected to loads for which they have historically not been designed. In addition, there is the feed-in of wind energy in the north. The required net expansions will have an increasing effect on investments and hence on the pricing of electricity in the future.

8.4 Electric Power in Developing Countries

The commodity electricity looks different in developing countries. To illustrate this, let us take a look at an example from Indonesia. Here too, there are power stations which use different energy sources. Here too, there are different voltage levels for transmitting and distributing the electric power, since the laws of physics are the same all over the world. There is, however, a difference: consumers demand more electricity than the production side can deliver; therefore, it is not always certain that the demand can be met by the available supply. Demand is not always same; there are peaks at certain times – toward evening, for instance, when people come home from work and switch on their television sets and their lights, or at mid-days in summer, when air conditioners are in high demand. At these times, the electrical output demanded by consumers is greater than what the power stations can make available. Therefore, compensation output must be provided, and there are several different ways to do so. In Indonesia, the consumer does not buy electricity, i.e., a certain number of kilowatt hours, but rather a given maximum output of kilowatts which may be used at peak times. Technically, this is quite simple. A sealed cut-off is installed which is activated as of a given power intensity, i.e., when the output level purchased has been exceeded, and interrupts the flow of power. For more output, the cut-off must be exchanged – and the cost for that is appropriately high. In industrialized countries too, there are cut-offs which limit the power in lines, only here, the limitation is not used to ration use, but only to protect the electric wiring in the house from an overload, which could cause a fire. In some countries, such as India or China, demand and available output are brought into line by not providing electricity to all consumption areas at the same time. There are shut-down schedules, and everybody knows at which times there will be no power available. That way, consumer demand is adapted to the available power station output.

8.5 The State Steps In

The price of electricity – and also of gas and other energy sources – is not always the market rate. Energy is special – in all countries of the world governments use the energy sector for their various political objectives – be it as an additional source of income for the treasury via energy taxes or other taxes, be it is as a political goodwill tool toward the voters, in the form of low energy prices, or be it as an additional incentive to establish industry in under-developed areas. However, the price of energy is also determined by political considerations, for reasons of supply security. For instance, Germany long maintained a coal subsidy at a high level for reasons of supply security, although coal could have been had more cheaply on the world market. Several figures should demonstrate the significance of energy for the German Treasury. In 2006, the country's total tax revenue from energy-related sources amounted to about €44 billion, according to Finance Ministry data. Of that, approx. 90% was accounted for by taxes on oil and natural gas, and the remaining 10% by taxes on electric power. In addition, there are local concession levies.

In some countries of the world, there is a split electric power rate, with private consumers buying electricity at below production cost, while industrial purchasers must pay excessive prices, compared with the production costs.

The procurement of energy resources and the development of energy systems are frequently subsidized. In Germany for example, both the federal government and the governments of the coal-producing states long paid subsidies for the extraction of hard coal, and more recently, renewable energies have received considerable start-up help through the Renewable Energies Law. It forces grid operators to accept electric-power feed-ins into the grid from renewables at any time, and thus reduce the power output at other power stations in exchange. However, since electric power from photovoltaics and wind energy is substantially more expensive today than that obtained from coal or nuclear energy, the difference is passed on to all electric power consumers, under the Renewable Energies Law. Even if that is not a subsidy in the strict legal sense, because the money does not come from the state, it is ultimately a politically imposed measure, since it is dictated to the power companies by law.

In the area of grid-bound energy sources, the state also intrudes into the market at another point. General principles for pricing for private customers are established by ordinance. If a consumer has decided in favor of a given rate, for example, he or she can pay the same as all others who have also chosen that rate. The provider may not distinguish between consumers who live in the inner city, where supply expenses are generally lower because of the higher connection density, and those who lives in remote rural areas and need long pipes or power lines. In countries where the electric-power markets have not been deregulated, the state participates in electric-power production and distribution via its own companies. An example is *Electricité de France* in France.

Although the European Union has no authority over energy under the Maastricht Treaty – each country still has full responsibility here – it nevertheless intervenes in the energy market. On the one hand, it is responsible for environmental and climate issues, including emissions from power stations. On the other, it sees electricity and gas as tradable commodities like any other, and has therefore for years been consistently pushing the introduction of deregulation of the gas and power markets, in accordance with the guarantee of free trade under its statutes.

8.6 What Does Electricity Cost?

The cost of energy becomes most apparent at the gas station, when it has to be paid directly. On the other hand, it is more

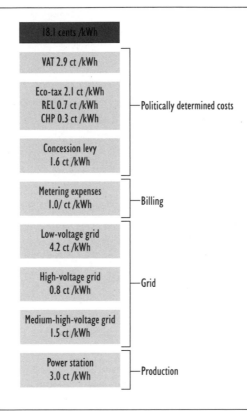

Figure 9 Itemized breakdown of expenses per kilowatt hour of electric power for a German household with moderate consumption (approx. 4,000 kWh), (as of fall, 2007)

difficult to say how high the natural gas or electricity bill is, for it is billed monthly at the same rate, and the customer becomes aware of the absolute amount, or the price per energy unit, only when the annual settlement is carried out. Moreover, it is interesting on the basis of the above discussion what the components of the prices paid by the consumer are. Figure 9 breaks down the average kWh price of approx. 18 cents.

The real production costs, including sales expenses, are only 3 cents per kWh. Another 6.5 cents pay for the grid, the use of the high-tension power lines, and distribution in the medium and low-voltage grids. The cost of metering electricity, i.e. of the meter itself and of reading it, also add up, at 1 cent per kWh. So: the kWh at the electrical outlet in the consumer's living room should be had for about 10.5 cents, correct? No, because on top of that, there are the government-imposed surcharges. In Germany, for example, there is the so-called concession levy, which the municipality gets for permitting the power company to use the right of way through town – i.e., to run their power lines above or under the streets. The amount of the concession levy depends on the population of the locality: it is 1.32 cents per kWh for household electric power in communities with less than 25,000 inhabitants, and 2.39 cents per kWh in cities with more than 500,000 inhabitants; the nationwide average concession-levy payment is approximately 1.6 cents per kWh. The levy on electric power charged to industrial customers is less. Here, the idea has been to strengthen the competitiveness of business, therefore the levy has been set at different levels for different customer groups.

A concession levy also has to be paid for gas, for the same reasons. Another government surcharge on the price of electric power is levied to promote the cogeneration of heat and power (CHP), which supports particularly efficient power stations that produce district heat and electricity at the same time. Then there are the payments due under the Renewable Energies Law (REL), which supports the feed-in of electricity from wind, photovoltaic, hydroelectric and other renewable power systems. The federal government also collects the "Eco-Tax" on electric power, which, however, is not in fact used to benefit the environment. It was introduced when the Ministry of Finance faced additional expenditures to save the old-age insurance system. Finally, there is the value added tax (VAT), imposed on almost everything. All in all, these add-on payments account for almost 40% of the electric bill.

It may appear surprising that the share of real electric-power generation in the overall cost, i.e., the power-station expenditures, are so low. The reason is the age of the power-plant park. Its capital expenses have already been fully amortized. However, about 40% of the power stations will have to be replaced over the next twenty years. Half of these are in the planning stage, or have already been ordered. In the future, the share of power-station expenditures in the prices of electricity will therefore increase again, since the new systems have to be amortized. Increasing fuel prices, too, will cause this component to rise further, so that electric power will generally become more expensive in the future. This trend is also supported by developments in the area of grid expenses. Here, there are two countervailing trends. Under EU regulations, countries with deregulated electricity markets are to set up grid regulation authorities, to whom the companies owning the grids must disclose their cost calculations and their fees for transmitting electricity. This increased transparency is expected to push down grid costs. On the other hand, there is a growing necessity to extend the high-voltage grid, because of the differing grid loads described above and the additional feed-in of wind power. Investments in the replacement of over-aged plants are also coming up.

So far, we have discussed only the cost structure for private consumers in the energy industry, or "end-users." The second large group of customers consists of industrial companies, small tradespeople, and commercial and service enterprises. Here, economies of scale are more significant than for household customers. The higher the quantity of energy bought, the lower the specific price. For grid-bound energy sources, the important thing is the regularity of purchase. Purchase peaks should be avoided if possible, because they force the provider to maintain large reserve capacities, and they have to be paid for. Therefore, industrial companies try to keep their peaks as low as possible when they purchase energy. For electricity, major industrial enterprises are attached directly to the high-tension grid. They can buy their electricity more cheaply, because the distribution costs are not paid by the provider. For industrial buyers, the concession levies and Eco-Tax rates are substantially lower than for private buyers, as they are, too, for the surcharges on the power price under the Renewable Energies Law. Industrial buyers face international competition when they market their products. Even if energy costs make up only a few percent of overall manufacturing expenses, they are nonetheless a competition factor. They can be decisive in determining whether production is to be shifted to other countries or not. That is the reason for the differentiation in government support for the price of energy between customer groups.

The Run on Energy Stocks

9 The Race for Deposit Areas

9.1 The Geography of Deposit Areas

Nature has distributed the world's energy reserves unevenly. Some are found on all the continents; others in only a few regions. Figure 10 shows this distribution. Looking at the overall situation of available energy resources, with no breakdown by energy source, we can distinguish three groups:

1. The largest reserves are located in Eurasia – a very large portion of them in Russia – North America and the Middle East.
2. A moderate amount of reserves can be found in Africa and the Far East, including China.
3. Smaller reserves are located in the European Union, Central and South America and Australia.

Notably, one major industrial nation, Japan, has no major energy reserves at all of its own. It is dependent on imports for almost all its fossil and nuclear fuels needs.

If we look at the world's energy reserves broken down by type of energy source, a very different picture emerges.

The coal reserves are twice as great as those of oil and natural gas together. On the other hand, the picture is reversed on the consumption side. There, twice as much oil and gas are used worldwide, as coal.

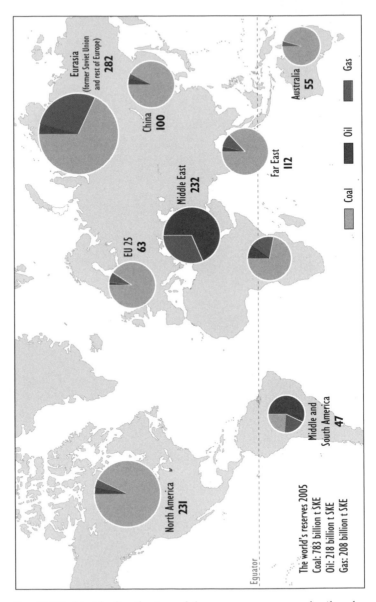

Figure 10 Worldwide distribution of the energy reserves coal, oil and natural gas

Coal, by far the most abundant energy carrier among the existing reserves, is found on all continents. That is the reason why only about 15% of the coal mined annually is traded between the continents. Oil, by contrast, is concentrated in only a few regions of the world. Here, the Middle East stands out. Central and South America are in second place. The third group, with considerably smaller resources, includes North America, Africa, the Far East with China, Russia and Europe. This distribution of reserves is responsible for major flows of world trade in oil – especially from the Middle East to all the other regions of the world.

Natural gas is also available on almost all continents; however, the deposits in the Middle East and in Siberia are far greater than in all the other continents. About 70% of all natural gas reserves are located in the strategic belt stretching from Siberia through the Caspian region to the Persian Gulf. In purely geographically terms, then, Western Europe is close enough to the major natural gas deposits to be able "tap into" them with pipeline systems.

The above explanations apply to the reserves of fossil energy sources. If we also look at the resource situation, it is slightly different, particularly as regards oil. Although the Middle East is in an outstanding position in the resources list too, because of its great potentials for secondary and tertiary extraction, there are also new major oil deposit areas in the oil and tar sands of Canada. Also the Arctic region – regardless of which country certain areas belong to politically – is another important deposit area for oil resources.

The renewable energy sources, too, are distributed unevenly in the world. The areas with the greatest solar-energy irradiation are along the equator, and global irradiation values drop as we approach the poles. For example, annual global solar energy irradiation in Central Europe amounts to only half what is measured at the equator. Moreover, the composition of the radiation changes. Only direct beams, i.e. those which travel parallel from the sun, can be concentrated by means of mirrors. That technology permits temperatures of several hundred degrees to be attained in solar-thermal power stations. Diffuse radiation, on the other hand, comes in at different angles, scattered by reflection off bright surfaces, or else by clouds; if that is all that is available for use, the temperatures will not exceed 90°C. While 80% of the incoming solar energy at the equator or even in California consists of direct sunlight, it is only 45% in Germany.

The distribution of wind energy in the world is different from that of solar radiation. There are two major wind-energy zones: the first is the trade winds zone, the second the zone of the westerlies. Central Europe is dominated by the westerlies, and is hence in an area with good wind-energy potential, on a world scale.

The nuclear fuel uranium has the unusual feature that only very small quantities, compared with fossil fuels, are needed to supply nuclear power stations worldwide. Uranium production amounted to only 42,000 tons in 2005. There are about 3 million tons of uranium reserves worldwide, largely located in eleven countries on all the continents. Australia is first, followed by Kazakhstan, the USA, Canada and South Africa. Other reserves exist in Brazil, Uzbekistan, Russia, Niger, Ukraine and China, with smaller quantities in some other countries. If we allow for higher uranium extraction costs, the amount of accessible reserves increases substantially.

In the following, let us examine the geographical location of the energy reserves and resources described, and then the possibilities of access to these stocks. And let us address the aspect of technical access first.

9.2 Technological Problems of Access

Hard coal is mined either by strip mining or in sub-surface mining. The mined coal is, if necessary, separated from non-combustible rocks, including sulfur, by means of a flotation process or in simple sedimentation basins. For this, large quantities of water are needed. The coal is then transported by rail, barge or, if necessary, ocean-going ship to the consumers. Hard coal is very easy to store.

Brown coal on the other hand is inferior in quality, as already explained in the section on trade. For economic reasons, it is used for electric-power generation in the immediate vicinity of the strip mines. It is transported there either by rail or directly by conveyor belt.

In world trade, it is often not possible to ship large quantities of coal directly to consumers. Take the example of the large coal belt in Central Siberia around Kansk and Achinsk. The coal is needed in the western part of the country. However, it has relatively low heating value and the only available transportation means, the railroad, is already hauling at full capacity. Similar problems exist also in other countries. In Indonesia, for example, the island of Java is the major population center, while the coal deposits are in Sumatra or other islands. Chinese coal, too, must be transported from the mining areas up to 2000 km to the main consumption areas. It is by far the largest item hauled by the Chinese railroad. All investigations into the question as to whether it would be cheaper to haul the coal to the consumers or to turn it into electric power at power stations near the mines and use high-tension power lines, have shown that hauling the coal was preferable for economic reasons. However, this may change in the future, since high-tension direct-current transmission with low transmission losses in the power lines has become cheaper.

As everyone knows, petroleum is transported by pipelines or in tankers. Oil refineries are available on all continents and in all industrialized countries and in the emerging-market nations. Nevertheless, investments in the refinery sector differ greatly between countries. In the USA, for example, this is the reason for the periodic lack of certain products, caused by a lack of refinery capacity, which must then be purchased from other refineries on the world market. Thus, not only crude oil, but also oil products are shipped worldwide.

Natural gas is largely moved through pipeline from the fields to the consumption centers. However, it can also be liquefied and transported at low temperatures in special tankers. This is necessary because not all consumer countries – Japan is a prime example – are accessible by pipeline systems. About 30% of world gas shipments are transported internationally over long distances. The rest is consumed "locally;" for instance, the gas from deposits in Norway and the Netherlands is consumed in Central Europe. Three quarters of the world's international natural gas trade moves by pipeline to the consumer countries, and one quarter is shipped as liquid natural gas (LNG) by tanker. The LNG proportion will increase, since Russia has announced plans to ship natural gas to the USA as of 2011.

The nuclear fuel uranium is shipped via the usual transportation routes from the producer to the enrichment plants and then the fuel-rod factories. Uranium is a low-intensity emitter. No expensive shielding or transportation security measure is therefore necessary to protect against radiation. Such shipments should not be confused with the transportation of spent fuel elements from temporary storage sites to reprocessing plants in Castor containers. These contain highly radioactive material which is the product of fission.

Technical access to renewable energies is being promoted in

the industrialized countries. They have developed photovoltaics facilities and wind systems of various types to series production. At present, the "cutting edge" of development involves large windmills for offshore operation 30 km from the coast. The objective here is to make use of the wind on the open sea, which is twice as abundant as on land. Emerging-market countries like China and India are trying to follow in the footsteps of the industrialized countries, helped by the fact that companies from the latter countries are setting up joint ventures with them, in order to open up their markets. For example, German companies are now producing wind-energy systems in Brazil and India. Developing countries have lacked access to this technology.

9.3 Economic Problems of Access

The technical access to energy sources is relatively simple. At least as far as the energy reserves are concerned, the necessary technology has been developed, and is in use. The situation is different as regards economic access to the energy stocks. As described above, energy is a commodity like any other. This means that, apart from some exception situations, energy is not shipped to other countries for below the world market price, even for political reasons. Like all other important products, energy resources are also sold for hard currency. Developing countries therefore also have difficulty obtaining economic access to energy, since they must have earned enough foreign exchange first; otherwise, they have no access. World trade in oil is carried out largely on a dollar basis. Therefore, the exchange rate between local currencies and the dollar also enters into the pricing. The prices for energy sources on the world market are established by supply-and-demand relationships. The demand is determined by the industrialized countries and a few newly prosperous emerging-market nations. If demand increases, the prices of energy also increase, to the disadvantage of the developing countries, which have only limited foreign exchange. Thus, economic access to energy is not open to all countries in the same measure. This will be even more the case in the future, with increased energy prices, due to the transition from today's cheap reserves to more expensive resources. With the grid-bound energy sources, such as natural gas and electric power, there is yet another hurdle. The grids are very capital-intensive, so that major investments must first be made for their construction. Since the technical prerequisites for that are moreover not fully available in developing countries, they are dependent on help from abroad, which must be paid for in hard currency. An electrical energy supply grid such as Germany's costs more than €2000 in investments per kilowatt of electrical output, when newly built. In the industrialized countries of Central Europe, exactly this one kilowatt in output from the power stations is what must be available for every citizen in order to assure the electric power supply. Considering for example that the gross national product per capita in the poorest countries according to the World Bank's rankings is about €2800, the significance of such an investment becomes clearer. It can be carried out only over the course of many years or even decades. Looking back historically, the electric power supply system in Central Europe, too, was built up over a period of at least two decades. For developing countries, it must moreover be taken into account that the GNP figures are not earned in hard currency. However, the development of the energy supply can be paid only partially in local currency; the rest must be bought on the world market for foreign exchange.

In the past, the industrialized countries have always had economic access to all fossil and nuclear energy resources. However, this should not obscure the fact that here, too, obtaining the financial means for major investments in energy supply has not always been easy. This leads on the one hand to the tendency for energy supply companies to merge, in order to become financially more powerful. On the other hand, such new developments as offshore wind parks, which involve greater technical and economic risk, have trouble finding the loans needed for investment capital. First of all, rising energy prices are a burden on the national economy. For almost three decades now, however, the German national economy has managed to compensate for the additional costs of rising oil prices by an increase in orders from oil-exporting countries. Here, the German national economy rather profited from other national economies, more than it "lost" money.

The economic accessibility of renewable energies varies widely, depending on the type of energy source, both in the developing countries and in the industrialized countries. Simple solar collectors for heating water can be produced and operated at local economic conditions in countries with a sufficient supply of solar energy. If these potentials have not yet been adequately developed, the reason is generally a lack of political leadership. More demanding technologies however, particularly for electric-power generation, involve considerably higher investment costs. Generation with the aid of photovoltaics still costs 35–40 cents per kWh in Germany, even for larger systems, twice what a home-owner pays for a kilowatt hour at his or her electrical outlet. Moreover, most developing countries probably lack the technical capacities to produce photovoltaic facilities, although such emerging-market nations as India can do so. This technology only has a chance there if it can be paid for in local currency. Even then, however, it is often not economical, compared with a simple diesel or gasoline engine attached to a generator. In the industrialized countries, where photovoltaics facilities must compete against extensive existing electric-power supply systems, their economic viability is a long way off. Nonetheless, photovoltaics serves a niche market large enough to build up photovoltaics industries which achieve good earnings. These include power for parking meters, telecommunications facilities, traffic-control systems and much more. For environmental reasons, many countries are promoting the launching of renewable-energies industries. The economic accessibility to renewables has therefore been secured in many industrialized countries by legal structures that force consumers to pay the higher costs involved.

Over the past ten years, wind energy has seen the greatest increase worldwide in the area of renewable energy. Wind energy can produce electricity more cheaply than photovoltaics. It is even viable in the emerging-market nations like India, since that country is not fully served by a central electric power supply system of power stations and grids. Many companies even produce their own electricity with the aid of diesel-generator facilities. Compared with this, the use of wind energy is cheap. Moreover, using the available diesel-generator facilities as a back-up in low-wind periods secures the energy supply of the company. For most developing countries, however, wind energy is economically very difficult to develop, although there are exceptions. Because of a lack of technical know-how of their own, and also the lack of production capacities, these countries are dependent on imports for a major share of these systems, and hence a foreign-exchange expenditure which is too great for them.

The use of nuclear power stations is economically characterized by the fact that their construction requires investments double or triple those needed for coal power stations of a comparable capacity. On the other hand, the fuel costs are very low, so that this form of power generation can compete with other energy sources. However, the high capital expenditure makes economic access to nuclear power feasible for only a few countries.

9.4 Geographical Problems of Access

Energy resources and reserves are often located in thinly populated areas with climatically difficult conditions. For example, large quantities of natural gas are extracted in permafrost areas of Siberia. The long gas pipelines for the supply of the West, stretching from Russia to Central Europe, cross large rivers, a particular technical challenge in springtime, when they are swelled with snow-melt water. Gaining access to the oil and natural-gas deposits at sea has also required the development of new technology. In 1973 for example, the Ekofisk field in the North Sea was developed in depths of 70 meters, with drilling platforms totaling 130 meters in height; later, the Statfjord field already required handling depths of 145 meters, with a platform height of 270 meters. Opening up of the Troll field off the coast of Norway in 1995 presented even more gigantic challenges, for the water was over 300 meters deep here. A gigantic platform 470 meters in height was assembled in Stavanger and then hauled to the field, the largest natural gas deposit area in Europe, some 80 km northwest of Bergen. There, it was lowered to the seabed by flooding its buoyancy tanks. By way of comparison: the steeple of the world's tallest cathedral, in Ulm in southern Germany, is 161 meters high. The investment costs of the platform of €110 million, demonstrate the high capital investment needed to secure natural-gas extraction.

9.5 Political Problems of Access

The battle for control of oil reserves and for the political access to them is already raging worldwide today. Even if there were plenty of other reasons for the wars in the Middle East, one important reason has been the question of safeguarding access to the region's hydrocarbon reserves. While the world's coal and even most of the uranium deposits are in the hands of the industrialized nations, a large proportion of the petroleum reserves are in their hands of predominately Muslim states. Experience has shown that while they also feel the economic need on the one hand to earn foreign exchange through the sale of oil and gas, they have on the other hand repeatedly used the sale of energy resources as a political tool in the past, and they will probably do so again in the future. For that reason, the countries belonging to the International Energy Agency (IEA) agreed after the two oil price crises of the 1970s to build up a three months' stock of oil, so as not to be vulnerable to short-term blackmail.

Each country pursues its own policy to maintain access to energy sources, particularly to hydrocarbons. The USA and its oil corporations are very directly involved in oil-producing regions. In order to ensure extraction and guard the transportation routes, they have also in the past relied on military means, if necessary. Europe on the other hand has tried as far as possible to pursue a balanced policy toward all important groups, and has depended on the laws of economics to ensure that it always has sufficient energy, i.e. it has been willing to pay higher prices. That EU policy, combined with the domestic supply base provided by the North Sea oil and gas fields, has to date proven effective, and Europe has also rapidly secured additional new suppliers of natural gas. The major such source is Russia. To date, it has considered its energy deliveries to the West in a purely economic context; there have been no politically motivated cuts in deliveries in the past. However, despite this contractual faithfulness, Russia's strategic environment could change in the future. Not only Western Europe, but also China, Japan and the USA are greatly interested in Russian gas deliveries. Concrete discussion for the construction of a pipeline to supply both China and Japan are currently being held, involving both planning and financing. Both countries are trying to elbow each other out to secure the major share of Russian gas, and are trying by means of promises of investment subsidies for the pipeline to secure such a share. The presidents of Russia and the USA have also agreed on the medium-term supply of Russian energy resources to the USA via LNG shipments. Strategic worldwide alliances could become an additional motivation for Russia to scatter its natural gas deliveries and to serve the world market. Russian export capacities will probably be limited by the fact that the country's economy also has a great need for its own for gas and oil. Hence, Western Europe will have to share Russian gas with still more partners in the future. The emerging-market nations, such as China and India, are trying to prepare themselves for the future. Their state petroleum companies are buying themselves into those oil-production areas where there are still shares to be allocated. Moreover, in 2005 they reached an agreement not to try to bid each other out of the market and thus push the prices up in the future, but rather to try to jointly ensure the energy supplies of both countries.

Access to nuclear fuels is very different from access to oil. Nuclear technology is a demanding technology which requires high security consciousness and a technically high safety standard. The prerequisites for building, operating and handling this technology responsibly do not exist in many countries. For political reasons, particularly those of supply security, India and China are increasingly trying to develop and build their own nuclear power stations. Their nuclear programs are motivated by the desire to be able to better meet the hunger for electricity in their large metropolitan areas.

Nuclear energy policy is international policy. On the one hand, there is a clear separation internationally between the peaceful and military uses of nuclear energy. On the other hand, however, the international community also depends on the safe operation of nuclear power stations in all countries. This may also be the reason that such countries as the USA or France are trying to push their nuclear technology for the development of nuclear reactors in emerging-market nations.

Energy security also means energy policy – both economic policy and foreign policy; we hope that it does not come to mean military policy, in the future. Realistically, we will have to recognize the fact that the world, today and in the future, has and will have an important sources of oil in countries and which must be considered difficult to access and politically risky.

Apart from Russia, presumably no country on earth would be capable of meeting its energy consumption requirements of all energy sources on its own. All other countries are therefore dependent on international access to energy deposit areas. Despite oil and gas deposits of its own, the energy dependence of the European Union is increasing continually. The EU is now dependent on foreign energy for about half its requirements. The limits of the energy resources in the North Sea is demonstrated by the fact that Great Britain has now switched from being a net exporter to a net importer of energy.

In the long run, the political accessibility of energy sources will probably be the decisive factor for the industrialized countries. For both technical accessibility and economic accessibility can be assured, even if rising energy prices are a burden on the economies of these countries.

We should hope that the international community manages to coordinate its energy interests in the future such that peaceful and not military means define them. The energy issue is one of the top items on the world's policy agenda – it was, for example, addressed at the G8 Summit in the summer of 2006 and 2007. There, the issues were safeguarding availability and risk reduction. Because of the different interests of the G8 member nations, which include both energy suppliers and energy importers, it was not to be expected that long-term solutions could be worked out during that first session. But it was a beginning.

10 The Oil Will Be Used Up Within Forty Years

Based on the 2006 consumption figures, 154,000 liters or 36,000 gallons – about seven large tank trucks-full of oil – are used up worldwide in one second. So when will the oil be used up?

The question as to when oil and other energy resources will run out is as old as their use itself. For forty years now, the prophesy has been that oil will run out within forty years – from the then current date. This may tempt us to believe that we really need not worry about how long energy resources will last, because experience has shown that, somewhere on earth, we will always find enough of it. But this view has a flaw; we have to look at all the aspects. It helps to distinguish between two concepts: that of energy reserves and that of energy resources.

With his diagram, McKelvey has provided a helpful breakdown of energy stocks (Figure 11), in which all the stocks of an energy resource are divided into "reserves" and "resources." One of the criteria for the distinction between them is knowledge about the deposit of the stocks. On the other hand, it is important to know how the technical and economic possibilities for the extraction of these stocks have been assessed. "Reserves" are those energy stocks the location of which in the world is known for certain or with great probability. Moreover, these stocks can be extracted given today's price levels and with today's technology; hence, it is certain that humankind has these energy-bearing materials at its disposal.

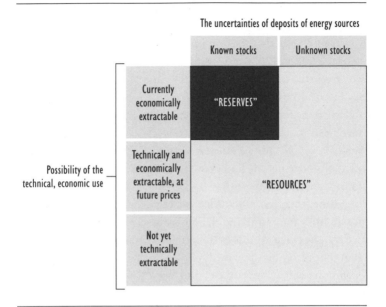

Figure 11 This McKelvey diagram subdivides all of the stocks of an energy source into "reserves" and "resources"

"Resources" – as defined in this system – are different. They are energy-bearing materials of which we know, or of which we assume with great probability that they are available at a certain place in the world, yet their extraction is either so expensive that it is unfeasible at today's prices, or else it is not yet possible technologically. These "resources" include for example those energy stocks which can be additionally obtained by switching to secondary or tertiary extraction (see also the explanations on page 17, on the question as to which energy forms we find in nature). Those "resources" also should be considered to include those suspected as existing in areas of the world which have still not been explored by test drilling for energy resources.

Let us clarify the division in "reserves" and "resources" with several examples. If we were to divide the stocks of petroleum which existed in 1930 into "reserves" and "resources," the North Sea oil would still have been a "resource," since it was not exploitable with the technology that existed then, it probably would not have been marketable at the price levels of the day, either, and finally, it could only be suspected that the North Sea contained oil at all, since no one had ever drilled for it. The oil shale deposits in Canada, on the other hand, have been well-known for a long time; their existence was considered certain. The technical possibilities for extracting them have also long been known. But to date, the price for this extraction has been considerably higher than that of oil on the world market, so that these deposits have been considered "resources" and not "reserves," according to this distinction. This has now changed, since at an oil price above $100 per barrel, oil shale could now be sold for a profit on the market. The Canadian oil shale has thus now switched from the "resource" to the "reserve" column.

Another speculative example is that of natural-gas hydrates, which are located in the continental shelf and continental slope areas of the oceans. Their sizes and locations are not known in full detail, but their total quantity is estimated to equal approximately that of all gas reserves known today. According to this system, however, they are "resources," on the one hand, because there is as yet no technology with which they can be extracted, and on the other because no cost assessment is therefore possible. The quantity of energy stocks available at a given price is therefore not a static quantum over time, but a dynamic one.

It is nevertheless helpful to define comparative figures. One useful one is static range, which is the ratio between existing energy reserves and annual consumption of the energy resource in question. It indicates how long reserves will last, provided the reserve situation and the rate of consumption do not change. And for oil, that range is approximately forty years – and it has been so for the past forty years.

Calculating the static range based on today's known reserves and consumption rates, we get the following rough figures:

- Hard coal   approx. 180–240 years
- Oil   approx. 40–50 years
- Natural gas   approx. 50–60 years
- Uranium   approx. 70–90 years.

An assessment as to which market price is to be assumed and which technology will be available involves a discretionary factor. As a result, the published figures for the reserves, and hence, too, the static ranges vary somewhat.

Static range does not mean that the energy source will not be available any more after the period in question is up. Rather, it depends on a variety of conditional factors, including:

- the development of the world's population
- the development of the world economy
- the technical development of energy use, i.e. energy efficiency
- the political availability of specific energy sources
- the price trend of energy sources
- the technical accessibility of new energy sources, for example the increase in renewable energies, or the production of liquid fuels from biomass, and
- progress in exploration and extraction technology for energy sources.

All in all, these factors mean that static range is subject to a constant process of change.

There are nevertheless limits to the quantities of available energy sources, some of which are beginning to emerge even today. For instance, geologists agree that the whole world has now been explored for oil deposits, given the means and the state of knowledge known today. We can thus begin to conceptualize when the oil extraction maximum could be passed – the so-called "peak-oil point," after which available stocks would decline in relation to expected future demand. Studies show that there is a good chance that that maximum point of oil extraction, related to the present reserves, will be passed in approximately fifteen to twenty years.

The overall situation of available energy sources can best be represented using oil. On the one hand, oil is the energy source which is quantitatively the most difficult to replace in the overall energy system; on the other, it is the energy source fraught with the greatest risks in terms of its political accessibility. The Paris-based International Energy Agency (IEA) has compiled a few statistics. Figure 12 shows not only the quantities of reserves and resources, but also their breakdown according to expected extraction costs, by today's standards. The OPEC reserves in the Middle East, which can be pumped for less than $15 per barrel, are the cheapest to extract. Other so-called conventional reserves in other countries can be extracted for less than $25 per barrel. If we cross the $20-per-barrel limit and assume crude-oil extraction costs of up to $50 per barrel for example, then many of today's "resources" can be reclassified as "reserves," an example being shale oil, as discussed above (page 110). The secondary and tertiary extraction of oil from today's deposit areas is also feasible at such a cost level.

Here, we should point out one difference: the $50 per barrel of extraction cost mentioned above should not be mistaken for the market price of $50 per barrel for the crude oil. In 2007, the market price averaged almost $75 per barrel, while extraction costs were below $30 per barrel. Thus, extraction costs of $50 per barrel would, granted the same profit to the oil-producing countries and the dealers, mean market prices of crude oil of about $100 per barrel – a level that has been far exceeded.

An analysis of the still available quantities of crude oil, as shown in Figure 12, is informative and perhaps also alarming. Expected worldwide consumption of crude oil through 2030 is equal to the quantity of cheap reserves that the OPEC estimates for the Middle East. On the other hand, the resources of oil shale represent five times the amount that has been consumed to date, and secondary and tertiary extraction promise an additional amount equal to three times the quantity already pumped.

Comparing these figures, it must be taken into account that oil consumption is developing exponentially. It amounted to over 30 billion barrels in 2007. In order to consume a quantity of oil equal to what has already been consumed since commercial production of oil products began would, at this rate of annual gross oil consumption, take only thirty-four years. But we also have to take into account the increases in oil consumption in the emerging-market nations of Asia, for example, which will lead to a run on oil. Demand will thus increase to over 30 billion barrels per year. This means that the time period will actually be shorter than thirty-four years.

The result of these considerations is that there are really more fossil energy sources – and also uranium – available than those who use the concepts of static range, or the "peak-oil theory," frequently indicate. However, extraction costs are doubling. It is also true that the hydrocarbons oil and gas, which, due to their environmental and utility characteristics, are in above-average

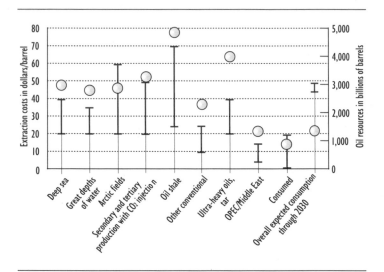

Figure 12 Reserves and resources of oil (circles), broken down by deposit area and extraction cost (lines) (Data source OECD-IEA)

The quantity of oil already consumed to date worldwide is shown for comparison.

demand, will not remain available for several centuries, considering the overall availability of stocks. These resources are limited; in the long run, it is thus worthwhile to try to develop and introduce additional new energy sources to the market, such as renewables or even nuclear fusion. The production of liquid fuels from biomass could also help ease the situation, to the extent that its potential permits; another possibility is the development of a hydrogen economy, where hydrogen fuel would be produced by splitting water molecules using nuclear power, or in the long run perhaps with electricity from photovoltaics. In the short run, however, all these options face the obstacle of commercial nonviability, in view of today's prices of energy.

The resource question is not a short-term, but a longer-term problem of energy supply. Here, "short-term" means a period of a few decades; "long-term" refers to time periods transcending generations, i.e., seventy years and more.

Energy Use and the Environment

11 Energy Conversion Creates Air Pollution

Environmental damage accompanies every energy source on its "journey through life:" from extraction and transportation to the conversion facility, such as the power station or the refinery, through its further transportation as a secondary energy source to the consumer, to its use by the "end-user." But what do we mean by the term "environmental damage?" And what environmental impacts are created, from the extraction of energy sources to their transformation to secondary energy, and thereafter during use by the consumer? And finally, how can we keep this environmental damage to a minimum?

11.1 Pollution and Types of Environmental Damage

Environmental damage is frequently defined as the negative effects upon, and changes in, the natural environment by physical, chemical and mechanical impacts. Polluting substances introduced into the environment, such as dust, micro-organisms, chemicals or radiation, can lead to environmental damage if they overtax the natural regenerative capacities of the environmental media, such as the soil, the water and the air.

Polluting substances are a major cause of environmental damage. These are substances which occur in the environment, and which, in dangerous concentrations, may have detrimental

Energy source	Technological sequence	Direct and possibly indirect environmental impacts	Indirect environmental impacts
Hard coal	• pit mining to depths of 1600 m • methane emission when venting the galleries • required stockpiling • major water needs for cleaning or sulfur removal • often, long transport routes	• methane emissions (in mining) • partial lowering of the earth's surface (mining damage) • space consumption and dust pollution from slag heaps • waste water from coal processing; for flotation, approx. 4.5 t/ ton of hard coal	
Brown coal	• strip mining to 500 m depth • lowering of groundwater tables • short transport routes (mainly conveyor belts; some railway transport)	• lowering of groundwater table • large consumption of space	• resettlement necessary • energy required to lower groundwater table
Natural gas	• long transport routes (e.g. Russia – 4000 km) • precipitation of heavy metals after extraction • offshore and onshore extraction • high energy requirement for compressors (approx. every 80 km) • transportation by pipeline	• methane emissions from leaks	• energy required for transportation via pipeline and compressors

Energy source	Technological sequence	Direct and possibly indirect environmental impacts	Indirect environmental impacts
Oil	• offshore extraction • transportation by pipeline or tanker • flaring of gas at extraction • long transportation routes	• methane release (at well) • tanker accidents	• energy required for refinery
Nuclear power	• low concentrations require large strip mines • long transport routes (Canada, Australia, Russia) • enrichment required • plutonium a by-product of fuel production	• space consumption for uranium and thorium mining • radioactive emissions from slag heaps (radon) • risk of release of radioactive matter in accidents	• energy required for enrichment
Renewable energies	• wind directly to electric power • the sun directly to electric power or heat • wood, mainly for heat production by burning • biomass processed to fuel	• monocultures for large industrial cultivation of biomass; also, use of fertilizers and pesticides required	• greater space consumption and material requirements than conventional power plants

Table 4 Environmental impacts of the sequence from the extraction of energy sources through the first transformation stage

effects on living beings and property. In terms of quantity and impact, pollution caused by energy use particularly involves emissions of harmful substances into the air.

For a precise evaluation, it is not enough to look only at single energy conversion systems, such as power stations or heating systems. While policy-makers often focus on the comparison of the environmental impacts of such single technologies, the processes of extraction and transportation of fuels also involve environmental damage, and must be considered. Table 4 shows an overview of these processes in an itemized list.

Hydroelectric and wind power occupy the leading positions in renewable energies. Neither causes anything like the environmental impacts that fossil energy sources do. Marginal effects include the – subjectively – changed view of the landscape due to wind turbines and the effects on plant and animal life in the areas flooded by hydroelectric facilities. Moreover, because of the unreliable availability of renewable energy sources, they must be supported by so-called back-up systems based on fossil fuels. Thus, they too indirectly cause environmental impacts.

Certain conversion systems, such as solar collectors, require a particularly high quantity of energy-absorbing material per unit of energy output. The extraction and processing of this material generally also involves environmental damage, which has to be taken into account when undertaking a factual comparison between the different technologies. Such examinations are carried out in the context of life cycle analyses (LCA), which are very detailed and extensive. We will therefore not be able to examine them any more closely here.

11.2 How They Get to Us

Air pollutants are emitted into the environment with exhaust fumes. Emission of pollutants is measured in units of quantity per unit of time, i.e., kilograms per hour, or tons per year. Emissions are legally regulated with established limit values.

Pollutants spread through the environment in accordance with weather conditions, in a process called transmission; in this process, they are diluted. In the air, they can react chemically with the atmospheric humidity and with each other, which can create secondary air pollutants, such as ozone. Sooner or later, they are deposited on the ground or on plants. If the rain washes them out, they may enter surface waters and the groundwater.

Pollutants emitted by smokestacks may be transported many hundreds of kilometers, while substances released near to ground level, especially in urban areas, usually do not travel very far. The long-distance transportation of pollutants means that countermeasures in the national framework are not enough. Germany thus "exports" a considerable portion of its polluting emissions to neighboring countries, depending on which way the wind is blowing; however, it also gets a considerable quantity in return from those neighbors. A very rigid clean-air policy in only one country would mean that that country would relieve its neighbors of some pollution, but would continue to "import" some of their emissions. The European countries have therefore made agreements to reduce cross-border environmental damage.

When pollutants impact on people, animals or property, we speak of the "immission" of those pollutants. The immission concentration is measured in milligrams per cubic meter of air, and is called the "swallow value." The intake of air pollutants or radioactive substances can occur via the respiratory tract, or through food and drinking water. Here, too, laws have been passed to impose maximum limit values.

11.3   Air Pollutants and Their Effects

A summary of the most important air pollutants, their effects and the remedies against them is shown in Table 5. The following explanations give a better understanding of the complex correlations.

Sulfur dioxide

Coal and petroleum contain sulfur, which is oxidized to gaseous sulfur dioxide (SO_2) in combustion. Medical examinations have shown that this causes damage in dry air only at quite high concentrations – it then leads to irritation of the bronchial tubes and the lungs. However, under the effects of sunlight and atmospheric humidity, SO_2 is further oxidized to sulfurous acid (H_2SO_3) and sulfuric acid (H_2SO_4). In connection with fine dust particles which are breathed in – so-called smog – aerosol droplets form, which are very tiny solid or liquid particles. Sulfur contributes to "acid rain" and hence to the acidification of the water and the soil, as well as to damage to buildings. In addition, sulfur compounds attack plants and contribute to forest damage.

Nitrogen oxides

Nitrogen oxides (NO_X) is the term used to describe both nitrogen monoxide (NO) and nitrogen dioxide (NO_2). They are among the undesirable by-products of combustion. There are two mechanisms which produce them:

	SO_2	NO_x	C_mH_n	CO	Dust	Radioactivity
Origin	S content of fuel	N content of fuel; high combustion temperatures	incomplete combustion; direct release		fly ash	natural sources; nuclear energy use
Trans-formation	H_2SO_3 H_2SO_4	HNO_2 HNO_3	Photo-oxidants (O_3)			
Effects on the human body	respiratory organs mucous membranes heart and circulation		respiratory organs partially carcinogenic and mutagenic	hampers O_2 transportation in the blood	respiratory organs	partially carcinogenic and mutagenic
Ecosystem	forest damage					
Property	structural damages					
Remedy	fluidized-bed combustion; flue gas sulfur-scrubbing	stage burners; de-NOx systems	high combustion temperature	O_2 excess	filter	filter dying down
		three way catalytic converter				
	acid rain; also synergetic effects with dust				condensation nuclei for acids	radiation exposure low

Table 5 The most important air pollutants from energy use and their effects

- The nitrogen contained in coal and oil burns to nitrogen monoxide (NO).
- Quantitatively much more significant is thermal NO_x formation, which occurs at temperatures above 1200°C. Atmospheric oxygen then disintegrates into two individual oxygen atoms which, in a series of chemical reactions, combine with atmospheric nitrogen to form nitrogen monoxide. This process occurs regardless of which energy source is actually being burned.

The nitrogen monoxide (NO) thus produced is relatively quickly transformed into nitrogen dioxide (NO_2) after leaving the chimney or the exhaust. Nitrogen oxides attack the mucous membranes of the respiratory organs, where they promote catarrhs and infections, such as bronchitis and pneumonia. They amplify the effect of sulfur dioxide.

Nitrogen oxides also react with atmospheric humidity to form nitrous (HNO_2) and nitric (HNO_3) acid which, like sulfuric acid, occur in the form of aerosols. These acids also contribute to "acid rain." Nitrogen oxides are also important precursor substance for low-level ozone.

Hydrocarbons

This term refers generally to all organic compounds which consist of carbon and hydrogen (C_mH_n). The important primary energy sources petroleum and natural gas, as well as all secondary energy sources like gasoline, fuel oil and liquefied gas produced from it, consist of low hydrocarbons with chain-shaped molecules. To some extent, they are emitted directly into the air, primarily from the tanks of motor vehicles, and when transferring fuel between containers. Considerable quantities are also released due to the evaporation of solvents, such as paints and varnishes – although this is not energy-related.

The main air pollutants, however, are the larger hydrocarbons. Under the effect of sunlight, they are also involved in photochemical smog formation, together with nitric oxide, which occurs particularly in summer, at times of high solar irradiation.

Carbon monoxide

Carbon monoxide (CO) is created during incomplete combustion, i.e. when there is an oxygen deficiency, primarily in the operation of motor vehicles and in coal heating in home stoves.

Its toxicity is due to the fact that it combines very tightly with the red hemoglobin that colors the blood – 200 to 300 times more tightly than oxygen – and thus displaces the oxygen; it is released from this combination again only very slowly, and thus hinders the transportation of oxygen in the blood.

Carbon monoxide is also involved in ozone formation, but is not itself the cause of it. It represents "wasted" energy, since the carbon atom has been incompletely burned, so that it has not produced its full heating value. It is therefore useful even for economic reasons to keep the generation of CO as low as possible.

Dust

Dust is created by operations in industrial facilities, such as cement plants, and during the combustion process, particularly when burning solid fuels, in the form of so-called fly ash. In industry and in power plants today, more than 99% of the dust is caught in filters. The finest dust particles, however, with diameters of several μm (1 μm = 1 millionth of a meter, or 0.001 mm, approximately the size of bacteria), can pass through most filters. Unlike coarser dust, this particulate matter of less than < 10 μm can enter into to the lungs through the respiratory tract. Its toxic effect is primarily due to the heavy metals, such as lead or cadmium, which it contains, since they can cause cancer. Moreover, other pollutants like hydrocarbons and sulfur or nitrogen compounds are inhaled on the surfaces of these fine invisible dust particles, so that they are transported into the lungs with the dust. Dust generally causes an increase in the number from of illnesses of the respiratory organs, like pneumonia and asthma.

Radioactive substances

The radioactive substances uranium and thorium present in coal are to some extent distributed as fine dust particles into the environment by way of power-station smokestacks. Their daughter products, metals like radium and radioactive lead, are inhaled along with the dust, and can thus enter the bloodstream. They are then deposited primarily in the bones, where the radiation can cause damage to health. Other radioactive substances, primarily such isotopes as Iodine 131, Krypton 85, Strontium 90 and Tritium (a name for Hydrogen 3), are also emitted by nuclear power stations, and are distributed in various ways through the body.

Radioactive substances can increase the risk of cancer, so that they have a similar effect to that of certain hydrocarbons and heavy metals.

In the next chapter, we will examine the possibilities of keeping harmful gas emissions in the energy-conversion process to a minimum.

12 Successes in Emissions Reduction

The previous chapter showed the necessity of keeping the output of air pollutants as low as possible. In the past, the industrialized countries proceeded to increase their energy output continuously without paying very much attention to the emission of air pollutants – as the emerging-market and the developing countries are doing today. Only once the effects could no longer be overlooked, about forty years ago, were measures taken to reduce dust emissions, and twenty years ago, to reduce the other air pollutants. Technological measures, some of which will be described here, have made this possible. They include on the one hand so-called "primary measures," which are carried out before or during combustion, and "secondary measures," which are implemented in the flue gas stream after combustion. Secondary measures are also known as "end-of-pipe technologies."

As a rule, primary measures are simpler and cheaper to implement than secondary measures. However, they are frequently not sufficient to achieve the specified limit values, so that both procedures must often be applied.

One primary measure widely used in the energy conversion process is stepped combustion. Its goal is, if possible, to prevent an increase to very high temperatures, which are largely responsible for thermal NO_x formation. For this purpose, the combustion takes place spatially in at least two zones. In the main combustion zone, it takes place sub-stoichiometrically, i.e. with oxygen deficiency – generally, the term "leaner-than-stoichiometric" is used. In the second, spatially adjacent combustion zone, air is added, so that here, the combustion takes place with an air surplus, or super-stoichiometrically; the more common term is "richer-than-stoichiometric." In small firing facilities such as home heating systems, the two combustion zones are implemented directly at in a single burner.

The flue gas desulfurization in power stations and large industrial plants is usually carried out by the so-called wet-scrubbing process, in which the flue gas is passed through a limy washing solution in a washing tower, so that the sulfur dioxide contained in it is chemically bound, and thus washed out. In ensuing stages, the washing solution with the sulfur is then turned into plaster, which is used in the construction industry. There are also processes in which elementary sulfur for the chemical industry is the end product.

De-NOx systems are facilities used for the denitrification of the flue gas in power stations or other large incineration facilities. They bring the nitrogen monoxide and nitrogen dioxide contained in the exhaust gas into contact with ammonia as a reducing agent, in the presence of a catalyst. The result of the chemical reaction is elementary nitrogen and water, both natural components of the environment.

The three-way catalytic converters used in internal-combustion engines operate without the use of any reducing agent, and are thus entirely different from power-station catalytic converters. Their mode of operation is based on the acceleration of the chemical reactions between the three exhaust-gas components. The three pollutants nitrogen oxide, hydrocarbons and carbon monoxide are simultaneously minimized – hence the name "three-way catalytic converter." However, this can be realized only at an air ratio of $\lambda = 1$ – which means that theoretically,

exactly as many oxygen molecules are available as are necessary for complete combustion (oxidation) of the fuel; in practical terms, the match cannot be exact, but must be very close,
within the range of the so-called "λ-window." For this purpose,
the fuel mixture in the carburetor and the fuel-injection system
are regulated prior to entry into the catalytic converter by means
of a measuring probe in the flue gas stream. Diesel vehicles have
a different mix of pollutants. Here, the problem is to capture
the soot particles and oxidize the carbon monoxide and the
hydrocarbons.

Dust particles are captured by means of various filter designs.
Technically speaking, there are very simple filters, such as
cyclones, which can be seen on the roofs of carpentry work-
shops. They look like metal cones, into which the exhaust gas
enters tangentially, and leaves again by way of a centrally placed
tube. The dust-filled exhaust-gas stream is made to rotate, and
the dust particles are driven outward by centrifugal force, strike
the wall, and slide downward. Even such simple designs allow the
separation of about half of all dust particles – but these are the
larger ones, not the fine particles that enter our lungs. These can
be separated out by tissue filters, simple versions of which are
used as paper filters in the fresh air supply in cars. For the filtra-
tion of the exhaust fumes of large heating systems, electrostatic
filters are used, which permit precipitation rates of up to 99.9%.
These filters are designed like electric capacitors operated by
high-voltage direct current. A skillful design makes it possible to
charge the dust particles electrically; they are then precipitated.

12.1 Successes in Air-Pollution Control in Industrialized Countries

In the industrialized countries, great successes in reducing air pollution have been achieved over the past thirty years. The summer smog episodes in the Los Angeles area, caused by the photo-oxidants emitted from vehicles, together with the intense irradiation, were the reason that as early as the 1970s, vehicles with catalytic converters were introduced to the U.S. market. Japan followed with three-way catalytic technology and, as of the middle of the 1980s, so did the European Union. The technology was continuously refined further, starting with the Euro-1 Standard; the internal-combustion engine is now subject to the Euro-4 Standard. Currently, soot filters are being installed in diesel engines. Catalytic-converter technology in vehicles has reduced the air pollutants generated in engines to about 5% of the previous amount.

Oil products for private consumption like diesel and light fuel oil are desulphurized Europe-wide at the refinery, because effective sulfur-scrubbing technology for small heating systems is not feasible in private homes. Heating systems, especially gas-operated condensing boilers, now cause such low emissions that they are for all practical purposes negligibly polluting.

The following emissions figures show the success achieved with these measures, with reference to the energy-related emissions in Germany as an example. These account for more than 90% of all emissions in their respective air-pollutant categories, except for dust.

— Carbon monoxide (CO):
    Reduced from 11.4 million tons in 1990 to 3.4 million tons in 2006
— Nitrogen oxides (NO_x):

Reduced from 2.7 million tons in 1990 to 1.2 million tons in 2006

- Sulfur dioxide (SO$_2$):
  Reduced from 5.2 million tons in 1990 to 0.4 million tons in 2006
- Dust:
  Reduced from 2.3 million tons in 1990 to 0.07 million tons in 2006.

Despite these impressive figures, the fact remains that the transformation and use of energy is not possible without environmental damage. Therefore, in environmental terms, the best energy use is energy which is not used. For reducing atmospheric pollution, as with other issues, energy savings are therefore at the top of the list of measures.

12.2 The Emerging-Market Countries Follow

However, in many metropolitan areas in the developing and emerging-market countries, the air is so polluted that it is a threat to the health of the people. In these countries too, new power stations are therefore being equipped with flue gas desulfurization equipment, and in the future will also have denitrification facilities. But not all the necessary technology is available in these countries; they are trying to obtain it by means of joint ventures and by learning on their own. They are also switching to new energy sources, as the industrialized countries did during the 1960s. In China for example, natural gas is increasingly being imported for heating and cooking in large cities. That permits dust emissions caused by burning coal, and the associated sulfur dioxide and smog formation, to be reduced considerably.

Today, three-way catalytic technology in internal-combustion engines and the oxidation catalytic converter in diesel engines is the state of the art, even in emerging-market countries like China and India. The drawback there is that the testing of the functionality of the installed catalytic converters is frequently deficient.

12.3 Air-Pollution Control Costs Money

Clean air is not free. Dedusting, denitrification and desulfurization in coal-fired power stations, for example, boost investment costs by 20%, and also mean additional operating expenses and additional energy requirements for the operation of the cleaning systems. The degree of effectiveness of the power stations drops. Ultimately, this raises production costs and means an increase in the cost of electric power on the order of 15 to 20%. At first glance, these figures may appear low, but their overall dimension becomes apparent if it is projected to the total of all required investments. During the 1990s, over €10 billion had to be invested in retrofitting existing power stations in the western German states alone, in order to fulfill the legal specifications for desulfurization and denitrification – dedusting had already been carried out. In a developing country, that kind of money would first have to be available in the national budget. In motor vehicles too, emissions reduction with three-way catalytic converters involves an expenditure of €400 and more per vehicle. Even if, in the industrialized countries, the increasing size and comfort, and the accompanying prices rise of vehicles mean that buyers are often not explicitly aware of the cost of catalytic technology, they pay for it nonetheless. For the more Spartan vehicles driven in developing countries, the additional expense for catalytic technology is definitely a consideration for the buyer.

The point is frequently made that environmental protection measures generate additional jobs and open up export opportunities, and are therefore ultimately of great economic use. These arguments are without question correct. However, how useful these measures are depends on the total extent of these advantages. A look at the development in Germany, for example, over the past twenty years shows a mixed picture here. The hoped-for export orders for refitting power plants abroad in the mid-1980s and early 1990s failed to materialize. Instead, other European countries developed and used their own technologies, while the emerging-market countries lacked the money for these imports. As a result, this branch of German industry suffered a sharp setback because of lack of orders, once it had completed the retrofitting program at home. Only at the end of the 1990s did the emerging-market countries start to install emissions-reduction technology by way of joint ventures – and they tried to keep as big a share as possible of the added value within their domestic economies, in order to save foreign exchange. In addition, while they would of course like to be able to master the most modern and effective technology, in many cases, they can achieve great emission reductions with less advanced and cheaper measures, for a better cost-benefit ratio, than if they were to import mature, highly advanced – and therefore expensive – European technology.

12.4 Controlling Greenhouse Gases

Finally, let us take a look at the differences between the reduction of air pollutants and that of greenhouse gases. Air pollutants are a direct – and, at high concentrations, very noticeable – burden on human beings and on nature, yet they affect only those world regions in which they are emitted; all measurement results show that – even with very high smokestacks – they do not leave their continents of origin. Greenhouse gases, on the other hand, have no direct physical effects, even at high concentrations – but they spread out very rapidly, worldwide. A second difference is that air pollutants can be converted into usable materials such as plaster, or into substances which occur in nature, even if that involves considerable expense. Greenhouse gasses, on the other hand, can for the most part only be reduced by using less fossil energy sources. We can therefore not hope for any reduction in greenhouse-gas emissions within a relatively short timeframe of two decades or so, as was accomplished in the case of air pollutants.

13 Waste Heat and Greenhouse Gasses

13.1 Waste Heat

Energy-conversion processes necessarily involve technical loss, so that waste heat is inevitably produced. Ultimately in fact, all the energy used for heating space is passed on to the environment via heat loss of the building or ventilation of the rooms, so that the "environment" and the atmosphere are heated. Measurements in winter show, for example, that the air temperature in large cities is up to 2°C higher than in nearby rural areas.

Another question is that of the longer-term effect of energy use on the earth's climate, particularly considering the growth of the world's population in mega-cities and the resulting growing energy needs. The energy shining down upon the earth from the sun is approximately 13,000 times greater than our present energy consumption. The local balance-sheet in major cities tells a different story, however: on average, they emit into the environment just as much heat energy per square kilometer per year as they receive from the sun. We do not yet know for sure what effect this has on the local climate.

13.2 Carbon Dioxide and Other Greenhouse Gases

The carbon dioxide (CO_2) formed by combustion processes is of special significance, because of its effect on the earth's atmosphere and the global climate. This is due to the fact that – like atmospheric water vapor, nitrogen dioxide, methane and ozone – it lets the sun's short-wave light rays through to the earth, but blocks the long-wave heat radiation – the infrared radiation – from leaving the earth. This is called the "greenhouse effect." The fact that these substances exist in our atmosphere in the first place is what has ensured a temperature at the earth's surface at which life became possible. Water vapor and natural carbon dioxide concentrations account for the major share of this natural greenhouse effect.

Large quantities of carbon dioxide are released by the decomposition of biomass and by the metabolism of living beings on land and in the sea. This is largely balanced out by an equally large consumption of CO_2 for the build-up of vegetable biomass, so that the natural carbon account is in equilibrium. However, that equilibrium is disturbed by the burning of fossil energy sources and the clear-cutting of forests. The burning of coal, gas and oil accounted for 8.2 billion tons of carbon worldwide in 2006, which means that 30 billion tons of CO_2 were released into the atmosphere. Worldwide CO_2 emissions amounted to almost 23 billion tons in 1990.

Human beings, too, are a natural CO_2 source. The air we breathe in has a CO_2 content of 0.038%; what we breathe out contains somewhat more than 4% CO_2.

The total quantity of CO_2 exhaled per human being daily amounts to 700 grams and more. With 6.6 billion people in the world, that means an annual total output of 1.7 billion tons of CO_2. If the number of people in the world increases to 8.5

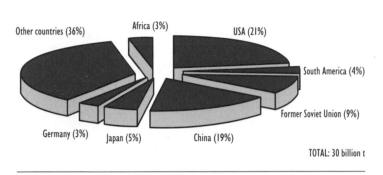

Figure 13 Worldwide CO_2 emissions in 2007, by country of origin

billion by 2025, as expected, humankind as a CO_2 source will be emitting some 500 million tons of CO_2 additionally every year. However, if we consider the increase in CO_2 emissions worldwide due to energy use, which amounted to 6.8 billion tons of CO_2 just within the past ten years, it is obvious that the direct effect of the increase in population is secondary.

The emitted carbon dioxide spreads out worldwide within the troposphere – the atmospheric layer up to about 10 km altitude – over the course of one year. Half of it stays in the atmosphere, the rest is taken up by the upper layers of the oceans, and from there passed on to the deeper levels of the sea over long periods of time. The continuous anthropogenic output of carbon dioxide raises its concentration in the atmosphere, so that the infrared radiation emitted from the earth's surface is reflected back again. That additionally heats up the mantle of air and the earth's surface.

The various fossil energy sources generate different amounts of carbon dioxide during combustion, due to their different chemical compositions. While hard coal and brown coal have very high carbon contents, petroleum and particularly natural gas also include considerable proportions of hydrogen along with the carbon, which also releases energy during combustion, the product of which is water. Their specific CO_2 emission per unit of energy produced is therefore lower. The CO_2 factors of important energy sources are:

Hard coal:	2.7 kg of CO_2 per kg of hard coal (equals 93 kg of CO_2 per GJ of heating value)
Brown coal:	3.1 kg of CO_2 per kg of brown coal (equals 109 kg of CO_2 per GJ of heating value)
Oil:	2.3–2.7 kg of CO_2 per liter, depending on whether it is crude oil, diesel, gasoline, fuel oil (equals 72–75 kg of CO_2 per GJ of heating value)
Natural gas:	1.8 kg of CO_2 per cubic meter (equals 56 kg of CO_2 per GJ of heating value)
1 kWh of electric power:	Mean value for Germany: 0.65 kg per kWh; from hard-coal power stations: 0.82 kg per kWh.

With natural gas, we have to take into account the fact that its principal component, methane, is also a greenhouse gas with an even higher specific greenhouse effect per molecule than CO_2. Even the loss of a few percent of the methane during the natural-gas extraction process would therefore nullify the advantage of the gas's lower CO_2 factor during combustion.

The CO_2 factors mentioned above make it possible to calculate the CO_2 emissions which a person causes by his or her energy consumption. Take a few examples: If a car uses 9 liters of gasoline per 100 km (26 mpg), that means 21 kg of CO_2 emissions (9 liters × 2.33 kg CO_2 per liter). The operation of a PC with accessories for seven hours uses one kilowatt hour of electric power, and therefore causes an average emission of 650 grams of CO_2.

In addition to carbon dioxide, other greenhouse gases are also released by human activity which, apart from a small share of the methane, has nothing to do with energy use. They include:

- Methane: from rice cultivation, animal husbandry, coal mining, natural-gas leakage, sanitary landfills, sewage plants
- Nitrous oxide: from the transformation of the nitrogen in the soil as a result of natural cycles and fertilization
- Ozone: photochemical formation from oxygen, nitrogen oxide and hydrocarbons
- Chlorofluorocarbons (CFCs): artificially produced propellants for foaming insulating material and as cryogens in refrigerators, air conditioners, etc.
- Halons (HCFCs): also artificially produced propellants for fire extinguishers and extinguisher systems.

Ozone has two different effects. The ozone in the stratosphere (12–50 km height) largely filters out the ultraviolet portion of the sunlight (290–310 nm wavelength). Destruction of the ozone layer in the stratosphere ("the ozone hole") by CFCs therefore means that the amount of UV radiation reaching the earth is increased. However, the ozone in the troposphere (up to 8 km height) is essentially formed photo-chemically from nitrogen oxides and hydrocarbons, as described in the section on air pollutants, above. This ozone functions as a greenhouse gas. Because of the ozone-destructive effect of CFCs in the stratosphere, their production and use have been banned by international agreements (the Montreal Protocol and subsequent conferences). Substitute substances have been developed.

The concentration of carbon dioxide in the atmosphere is measured continuously. It amounted to 315 ppm in 1958, and increased to 380 ppm in 2005, which equals a 0.038% share by volume of the atmosphere. At the same time, it was discovered that the mean surface temperature of the earth is rising.

There are fears that the temperature rise will cause changes in the atmospheric and ocean currents, and hence a shift of climatic zones. This would mean a global mean precipitation increase and a change in soil dampness, and, as a result, in vegetation. Some of the continental snow and ice masses could melt. As a result of these climate changes, weather anomalies, such as storms, droughts and cold waves could be expected more frequently. Moreover, there could be a shift in the location of good crop yields, and flooding of densely populated coastal areas.

A reduction of carbon dioxide emissions will be far more difficult to achieve than the reduction in air pollution has been. Although CO_2 could be separated out of the flue gases of power stations, home heating facilities, and even vehicles, that would involve very great effort, expense, and also energy. In particular, the question of how to "store" large quantities of CO_2 is unresolved. In the case of the air pollutants described above, transformation into other products, such as plaster in the desulfurization process, or into natural substances like nitrogen and water in the catalytic processes, is possible, but there are no such possibilities for carbon dioxide. The frequently discussed possibility of capturing the CO_2 and disposing of it in liquid or solid form in the deep sea, either through pipes or as "dry-ice torpedoes," is still only theoretical, and is questionable, particularly with regard to its ecological compatibility.

It is more realistic to use CO_2 for the secondary extraction of natural gas and petroleum, and to ultimately dispose of it by forcing it into empty wells. However, only a portion of the CO_2 generated could be "disposed of" in this manner. The only way to really reduce carbon dioxide emissions would be by switching to low-carbon or no-carbon energy sources – and by reducing energy consumption.

13.3 National and International Policies

Starting with the UN Conference on Environment and Development in 1992, an international process with the goal of reducing greenhouse-gas emissions was initiated, which climaxed with the conclusion of the Kyoto Protocol. In that agreement, 150 countries assumed the obligation to achieve certain reduction goals in their greenhouse-gas emissions during the period from 2008 to 2012, compared with the base year 1990. Developing and emerging-market countries were exempted from these reduction requirements, since they were recognized as having a catch-up need in terms of energy use, which would mean additional emissions. And although the United States promised in Kyoto to reduce its greenhouse-gas emissions by 7%, it has not yet ratified the agreement, for fear of too-high reduction expenditures and resulting disadvantages for its economy.

The European Union is a party to this Kyoto Protocol as a whole, and has agreed to reduce emissions throughout the EU by 12%. In an internal EU division of labor, Germany has assumed by far the largest share of this target, promising to lower its CO_2 emissions by 25% over the 1990 level by 2012, although this high reduction objective includes the effects of reunification. The shut-down of many industrial facilities in the eastern German states and the refitting of residential buildings with gas heaters instead of coal stoves, as well as the new construction of more efficient coal-fired power stations considerably reduced CO_2 emissions, without the implementation of any specific reduction measures.

However, as of 2008, it does not look as if it will be possible to accomplish the reduction goals set in Kyoto for 2012. One indication of that is the continuing increase in worldwide CO_2 emissions over the past few years.

In order to achieve the targeted reduction in global emissions of greenhouse gases, common cross-border measures for climate protection are to be implemented. The Kyoto Protocol provides for four mechanisms for achieving greenhouse-gas savings internationally, on the basis of free-enterprise principles:

1. *Bubbles*: These permit groups of countries to accomplish a goal jointly. To date, the European Union is the only group of countries worldwide which has chosen this method.
2. *Emissions trading*: Under this system, CO_2 certificates are issued. Some industrial plants may only emit as much CO_2 as they have certificates. If the plant does not fully use up its certificates, it may sell them to others; on the other hand, if its CO_2 emissions are higher than the amount of certificates it has, it must buy more certificates. Thus, market prices for certificates will emerge. This worldwide certificate trading system is to be introduced as of 2008. In order to launch the emissions-trading system, a certain quantity of CO_2 is to be certified as the initial value for each country in the Protocol, and each country is to issue a certain number of free certificates to its plants. Some nations have a surplus of

certificates as compared with their actual CO_2 emissions, due to their negotiating skills, or to a decline in economic activities – Russia being the prime example. They can thus sell their surplus of certificates internationally, and obtain additional revenue from them.

The European Union has obligated its member countries to introduce certificate systems of their own. In Germany for example, 2600 industrial plants are affected by this measure, including of course power stations and major industrial boilers, and also steel mills and paper mills. These 2600 plants generate about 60% of Germany's CO_2 emissions.

3. *Joint implementation*: This system makes it possible for industrialized countries to carry out projects for the reduction of greenhouse gases in other industrialized countries, and to have these investments credited to their own reduction targets.

4. *Clean-development mechanisms*: Like joint implementation, this system involves international projects, but between industrialized countries and developing countries, with the reductions credited to the accounts of the industrialized countries. Countries not subject to the CO_2 limitation measures, such as India and China, want to carry out projects like the construction of hydroelectric power stations, and profit through access to know-how and financial support from the partner industrialized country. That industrialized country would then profit by receiving CO_2 certificates, which it would hope to obtain at below the going market rate. Projects of this kind must be approved by an international certification agency created especially for this purpose. It is a bureaucratic process.

The first step toward the introduction of CO_2 certificates in the European framework was the issuance of free certificates to the facilities concerned by each of the countries. One difficult question that remains unanswered is how to handle efficiency increases and expansions of production. Increases in the efficiency of energy conversion mean less CO_2 emissions. That frees up certificates. The same happens if the companies reduce their production, or shift it abroad. Do the certificates previously assigned then have to be returned, or may they be sold on the market?

On the other hand, if a company expands production, it will need additional energy consumption and hence more certificates, which in turn makes production more expensive, and may restrict its competitiveness. If certificate prices are very high, economic activities could be hampered. It is thus hardly surprising that the rules of certificate trading are subject to constant discussion. Is also far from clear whether and how the existing certificate system can be incorporated into the international system after 2008, and whether emissions-reduction accomplishments previously achieved will then still be counted.

The price of a certificate traded for the right to emit one ton of CO_2 had increased to €20 by the end of 2007. Certificate prices at this level have an effect on the choice of the energy source. In view of the fact that large portions of the German and European power-plant park will have to be replaced due to age within the next twenty years, the question of the economic competition between the energy sources in light of the introduction of CO_2 certificates arises. For example, coal and coal-fired power generation will be made considerably more expensive by the certificates than power generation from natural gas. On the other hand, the additional demand for natural gas which this will cause could raise the price of natural gas so much that coal would then be competitive again for power generation. The price of electric power per kilowatt hour will in any case become more expensive for everybody due to the certificates. Considering for example that 820 grams of CO_2 are charged for the generation of each kilowatt hour of electricity from hard coal, a certificate price of €20 per ton of CO_2 means a rise in the price of power generation of about 1.6 cents per kWh. This is equal to one third of expected electricity-generation costs without CO_2 certificates, so that it is a major economic consideration. On the other hand, however, companies will actually only have to buy a small portion of the certificates they will need. By far the largest part will be issued to them free of charge as their initial contingent.

13.4 The Cost of CO_2 Reduction

The reduction of CO_2 emissions by efficient energy use or by the increased switch to renewable energies costs money. In particular, there are a large number of possible measures for lowering CO_2 emissions. For example, an improvement in the energy efficiency of home appliances could permit the use of less electric power, and thus lower emissions. An improvement in the energy conversion efficiency of power stations or heating systems could also contribute to fuel economy and reduced CO_2 emissions. The restructuring of processes in industry could also allow for lower consumption of fuel oil, gas or electric power, and hence lower emissions.

Electric power is produced with zero emissions of CO_2 by nuclear power plants, wind energy, and solar systems. The question therefore arises as to which measures can and should be tackled first. The cost aspect is one important criterion. From the point of view of cost-benefit considerations, we should always first try to avoid generating that ton of CO_2 which can be avoided at the lowest cost. Let us look at some examples which apply to conditions in Germany and which show the scope of possible measures:

In the area of electric-power generation, the degree of effectiveness of existing fossil-fuel-fired power plants was improved by implementation of about 180 different measures between 1993 and 1995, the equipping of turbines with new blades being the most important. That reduction in specific fuel consumption caused CO_2 savings of almost 7 million tons per year. Another 240 measures were carried out in 1996, which resulted in CO_2 savings of about 2 million tons per year. If the expenses that these measures involved are assigned exclusively to the account of CO_2 reduction – which they should not be, since those expenditures actually also prevented other emissions, which were not emitted since the corresponding fuel was not burned – it turns out that a ton of CO_2 could be "saved" with less than €15 in expenditure. That same amount of CO_2 could also have been avoided by generating the electric power with windmills. To do so, it would be necessary to install 31,000 windmills with 2 MW of electrical output each at coastal sites, assuming a duration time of 2200 hours per year. The cost of electric-power generation by wind energy amounts to 8 cents per kWh, twice the cost of electricity from conventional power stations. For these additional costs, CO_2 savings of 0.65 kg per kWh are obtained. The specific CO_2 reduction expenditures per ton are €60, and therefore higher than the CO_2 savings from refitting power plants.

Private consumers can achieve CO_2 reductions still more cheaply than the above examples by buying such new household equipment as hot-water boilers, washing machines, or freezers. They use less energy than their predecessors, although the cost of the equipment has increased only insignificantly, or is even paid for by the lower energy consumption. In this case, the CO_2

reduction is *de facto* free. If it is possible to use energy-saving light bulbs instead of traditional bulbs, the 6000 hours of operating time will cost no more, at €10, than the six light bulbs that would otherwise be needed. The lower electricity consumption results in lower CO_2 emissions; this reduction, too, is thus attainable at no additional cost.

A Ray of Hope: Energy Efficiency and Renewable Energies

14 Saving Energy

The best energy source is the one that is not used, since it need not be extracted or used for power generation, and causes no atmospheric pollution or greenhouse-gas emissions. We talk about saving energy in everyday life; yet it is useful to distinguish between two conceptual definitions: energy savings and rational energy use, or energy efficiency. Energy saving means the consumption of less energy by changed behavior. Examples include:

– reducing room temperatures and dressing more warmly instead of heating
– cooling room temperature down less when air conditioning
– driving less, or, when driving, avoiding unnecessary acceleration and braking
– heating and lighting only those areas needed.

Most people don't like energy saving; they often see it as a restriction on their personal freedom. They would rather reduce their energy consumption through greater energy efficiency – by the more rational use of energy. Here are some examples:

– improvements in the efficiency levels of heaters, engines and vehicles
– improved power-station technology
– reduction of the need for heating in buildings through improved insulation.

In all these cases, the use of "energy-eating gadgets" is not restricted, but the gadgets do what we want them to do without using so much energy.

The motivation for energy savings and for increased energy efficiency is ultimately the same in all areas of application, but the objectives are pursued at differing levels of intensity. A few people save energy out of idealistic conviction; the rest of us do so only to save money; our goal is to cushion or compensate for rising energy prices or ancillary expenses related to the emission of air pollutants and greenhouse gasses – such as the prices of CO_2 certificates. In industry, increased competitiveness due to the reduced cost of this expense item is an additional factor. This motivation always takes effect when an energy consumer has to pay for needed energy and at the same time has the possibility to take measures to manage energy more efficiently. However, the latter is not always possible. For example, office space is frequently rented at a fixed price per square meter, including energy expenses. There is an additional hurdle for rented residential apartments: since the tenants bear the cost of energy by having it passed on to them, the landlord has no particular interest in energy-efficient heating systems, nor in improving the insulation of an existing building, other than its possibly increased market value.

The tenant on the other hand has no control over changes in the structural substance of the building designed to achieve greater energy efficiency. Even if he is willing to make investments by agreement with the landlord at his own expense, he often does not know how long he will be living in the building, and hence whether that investment will pay off for him. Here, other motivation mechanisms are needed, in addition to the cost factor. In Germany for example, the newly established "energy pass" requirement for buildings is designed to serve that purpose. It provides information about the thermo-technical standard of a building, and shows a potential tenant what heating expenses he will be likely to face.

14.1 Past Successes

Since the two energy-price crises of the 1970s, when oil prices tripled within a very short time, a variety of measures for more efficient energy management and for better insulation of buildings have been taken. One reason for that was that energy-savings made economic sense, given the higher price of energy. The other was that they were stipulated by national and EU-wide regulations, the most important of which were:

- minimum requirements for insulation standards in buildings and energy efficiency in heating systems
- standards for the emission of air pollutants
- for rental apartments, the requirement that heat use be billed according to consumption, and that new home appliances and also new cars be labeled to show their energy consumption, to permit potential buyers to compare products in terms of their energy efficiency
- financial support for particularly energy-efficient systems which produce both electric power and district heat or industrial process heat at the same time.

All in all, these measures were the reason that a so-called decoupling of economic growth from primary energy consumption took place. During the 1960s and '70s, primary energy consumption grew in step with the gross national product, by almost the same percentage; starting in the 1980s, there was lower growth in energy consumption, in spite of further increases in the gross national product. Over the past ten years, primary energy consumption has stagnated, while the gross national product has continued to grow slightly. This decoupling has been achieved by energy savings, increased energy efficiency, and also by a restructuring of the economy. While the high-input production of raw materials like iron, building materials and chemicals were the basic factors affecting the structure of the economy, the technical and non-technical service sectors, such as office and information technology and social services, have made increasingly large contributions to the gross national product over the past twenty years. They are less energy-intensive, and thus contribute to the decoupling of primary energy consumption from overall economic growth.

14.2 Possibilities for Improved Economy and Efficiency

The measures for thrifty energy management can be divided into three groups:

– behavior-related measures
– organizational measures
– investments.

The behavior-related measures include for example steady and farsighted driving habits in both automobile and truck traffic, rather than hectic acceleration and "gap jumping." A test with two truck drivers on a 1500 km stretch showed, for example, that the faster driver had only a 7% time saving over the more foresighted, moderate driver, but that the latter used 30% less fuel. In many cases, short-distance drives with cold engines can also be avoided by changed behavior. Behavior-related measures in the area of heat use include adjusting the heating to more moderate levels, heating rooms, particularly business premises, in accordance with need, and appropriate ventilation. Experience has shown that lowering the temperature of a room by about 1°C makes an approx. 5% difference in energy costs. Behavior-related measures do not cost money; on the contrary, they save energy expenses.

Organizational measures include, in the area of traffic, vehicle maintenance activity, such as oil and air pressure, and engine tuning, the removal of roof luggage racks when not needed, and of excess weight in the form of unnecessary items in the trunk or load area. Transportation can also be reorganized so as to shift loads from road to rail or to ships, where the same transportation service can be rendered for less expenditure of energy. Organizational measures in industry can save energy by only heating and lighting factories and offices while people are working in them. Energy costs can also be decreased by ensuring that the power-consumption peaks are not too high. One should also check to see whether all equipment in operation is actually being used. Industrial consumers of power, unlike household customers, must also pay for the maximum kilowatt output they need, so that consumption peaks are very expensive. Organizational measures can be carried out at relatively low cost. However, they should be implemented so that they are continued over the long run, to achieve the desired reduction effect.

As a rule, investments are only carried out if they make sense from a business point of view. The reasonable payback period, upon which a company bases its other investments, is normally taken as the criterion. For companies facing tough competition, the specifications for the payback periods are very short, often less than a year. As a result, not all possibilities for energy savings are exhausted. Such investments include the acquisition of new, thriftier vehicles, the replacement of old and often over-sized boilers, the plugging of leaks in compressed-air systems, and improvements in the insulation of buildings. The government could also contribute considerably to energy savings in the traffic sector if it were to succeed in eliminating certain congestion points on freeways. Vehicles in traffic jams use up energy without getting any use out of it.

Let us now discuss some of the existing potentials for further increased energy efficiency: The continuing progress toward an information society is the reason why modern households and companies are equipped with a variety of appliances, information and office equipment, with audio and video equipment, television sets, cameras, telephones, PC accessories and coffee machines. Often, for reasons of convenience, they are, technically speaking, not switched off completely, but rather run in idle mode, or stand-by. Battery chargers stay plugged into the electrical outlet even if no cell phone is being loaded. Many other devices, such as television sets, are still on stand-by, even after they have apparently been turned off. Stand-by consumption of any one device is low; nonetheless, the combined electrical energy required for the many millions of such devices is considerable. Although the reduction potential here has long been known and to some extent even realized, recent investigations have revealed that in Germany, a total of 18 terawatt-hours (TWh) are produced for these idle and stand-by operations – a total of 3% of electric-power generation. That amount is equal to almost half of Germany's total installed wind-power output in 2007, or the power production of two nuclear power plants. Of course, the losses caused by such stand-by operations cannot be eliminated entirely. A PC or printer cannot be switched off every time the operator takes a break. However, TV sets and audio equipment can be switched off overnight, and recharging devices can be shut off when not needed. Investigations show that about 40% of the electric-power consumption mentioned above is available as a reduction potential through behavior-related measures.

The light needed per square meter of floor space or per cubic meter of room volume can be generated in various color qualities and at various levels of use of energy. For technical reasons, the transformation of electrical energy into light basically involves a low level of energy efficiency. An electric light bulb converts only 5% of the electrical energy supplied to it into light, halogen lamps boost that to almost 10%, and peak efficiency – 25% – with fairly good light color is achieved by compact fluorescent lamps with modern electronic adapters. Only high-pressure sodium-vapor or mercury-vapor lamps for the illumination of roads or large industrial halls achieve higher energy use rates; however, they have the disadvantage that their light color is not suitable for residential areas, offices and workrooms. At the present price of electricity, it always pays to exchange electric light bulbs for compact fluorescent lamps, and older fluorescent lamps for modern lighting appliances, in spite of the initially higher investment costs. The energy savings and the accompanying reduction in greenhouse-gas emissions and air pollution are free extras.

There is a very great potential for heating rooms with less energy. That is the reason for recent German legislation mandating that new buildings and even major renovations of old buildings provide certain standards of insulation which, however, are unfortunately still not always being met in practice. That happens because the insulation must only be documented on paper in the building application, but the technical implementation of the insulation measures is not checked; that is up to the clients. With regard to heat consumption, there are also considerable differences, depending on the date of construction of a building.

Notably, very old buildings as a rule have better thermal protection than buildings built when oil prices were low, during the 1960s and '70s. After about thirty years, buildings generally need to be thoroughly renovated. That is when the thermo-technical rehabilitation of the building shell is most feasible, and when it can be done at the lowest additional cost.

The savings potential can be shown most clearly by a comparison of buildings with different thermo-technical standards. The heating energy requirement is normally indicated in kilowatt hours per square meter of living space per year, or else in fuel-oil equivalent (or natural-gas equivalent) per square meter per year. Comparing the values for detached houses, the following order emerges, depending on the insulation standard:

- *Non-rehabilitated buildings built before 1970:* They need about 20 liters of fuel oil (or 20 cubic meters of natural gas) per square meter of living space per year for heating; for particularly poorly insulated buildings, that can go up to 30 liters.
- *Buildings built in West Germany according to the legal stipulations passed in 1982:* They need about 15 liters of fuel oil (or 15 cubic meters natural gas) per square meter of living space per year for heating.
- *Buildings built according to the stipulations passed in 1995:* They need about 9 liters of fuel oil (or 9 cubic meters natural gas) per square meter of living space per year for heating.
- *Low-energy houses, i.e., houses with insulation performance exceeding the requirements of the Energy Savings Law by 30%:* They need only 6 liters of fuel oil (or 6 cubic meters natural gas) per square meter of living space per year for heating.

In all these cases, a dwelling of equal dimensions was assumed, for the heat requirement of a building is determined by various factors. The most important is the thermo-technical design of the shell and the windows. Second is how ventilation is handled. If the windows are permanently tilt-opened or ajar, the air exchange can be four times as great as necessary for reasons of health, which wastes a great amount of heat unnecessarily. An additional important factor is the relationship between the outer surface of the building and its living space, i.e., its dimensions. The more compact a building is, the less heat energy it needs.

The latest developments are moving in the direction of the so-called "three-liter house" and the "passive house." The three-liter house is a very thrifty low-energy house with a heating requirement of 3 liters of fuel oil per square meter per year. Passive houses have even lower specific heat use than that – a building using less than 1.5 liters per square meter per year qualifies as a passive house. About a thousand such houses have already been built in Germany. In order to maintain this low energy-use level, controlled ventilation is important. Air exchange must be no greater than necessary, so that no heat is lost unnecessarily. Generally, the ventilation systems are designed with heat recovery, to limit these heat losses. The heat in the air passed out of the building is transferred to a heat exchanger to heat up the air entering the building from the outside. While in older buildings, the heat losses through the walls and windows are the key factor, in low energy houses, the ventilation losses assume that same role. Current developments are moving toward energy systems controlled by networking the windows and the heating systems. Such "intelligent houses" will be able to recognize when windows are opened and the radiator under a window is on at the same time.

Note that the consumption values stated above reflect only

the so-called heating energy requirement, or the amount of heat which must be brought into the building to maintain the desired temperature. The conversion of the energy from the fuel oil or the natural gas to heat energy for the building in the boiler can still involve losses of up to 10%, depending on the heater installed. The energy consumption of the residents is then increased by this amount.

The figures show that a single-family home in which for example an average of 120 sq. m. of living space are heated, may, depending on a thermo-technical design, need either up to 2400 liters of fuel oil per year for a non-renovated old building, or only 700 liters of fuel oil per year for a low-energy house, plus the conversion losses in the boiler of 10%. This means a difference in the energy bill of €1200 per year, at a heating-oil price of 65 cents per liter. Multiple dwellings have a 10 to 15% lower heating energy requirement for a given technical design, because they have a more compact ratio of outer surface to living space.

Buildings are "energy-conversion units" with very long life spans. It is therefore important to develop the energy reduction potential in the existing building stock as a matter of priority, even if improvements in insulation standards can be achieved more easily in new buildings. Experience has shown that it is possible to perform a basic renovation of buildings built during the 1950s so that they comply with the Thermal Protection Ordinance of 1995. Their energy consumption is then halved. Given today's energy prices, these measures also make good business sense. Moreover, the German government provides favorable investment credits to promote greater thermal protection. Reduction potentials in the area of buildings need periods of several decades to be realized. If we assume that all buildings built before 1990 will be renovated within forty years, that would mean a potential reduction on the order of 30% of today's heating requirements.

In terms of Germany's overall primary energy needs, that would amount to a 6% reduction. The thermo-technical rehabilitation of the building stock is therefore a key component of the future energy-supply picture.

14.3 The Conflict between Consumer Behavior and Energy Efficiency

While buildings, electrical equipment and vehicles are being improved energetically, consumer demand for space to be heated, equipment to be run and kilometers to be traveled is increasing. For that reason, not all technically possible reduction potentials can in fact lower energy consumption. Let us take a look at four examples:

– Between 1995 and 2003, the number of passenger-kilometers travelled in cars in Germany increased from 740 billion to 820 billion km. At the same time, the average specific consumption of the vehicles dropped from 9 liters to 8.4 liters per 100 km (a rise from 26 to 28 mpg), thanks to improved technology. But as a result of this increase in travel, total fuel consumption nevertheless increased by 3% during this period.
– During that same period, from 1995 to 2003, the stock of living space in Germany increased from 3 billion to 3.38 billion sq. m. Because of better insulation, consumer energy consumption for heating dropped from 19.6 liters of fuel oil per square meter of living space to just over 17 liters. But as a result of the overall increase in living space, total energy consumption was not reduced in absolute terms. The same also applies if we look back over a longer period of time, for instance from 1980 through 2003.

- The energy efficiency of electrical equipment is also improving, but at the same time, households have ever more electrical equipment. The specific electric-power consumption was reduced by 11% for audio, video and data processing equipment during the period from 1997 to 2005; however, the stock of equipment increased by 13% during that period. Overall electric-power consumption thus increased slightly for this segment. The same also applies to "white goods" – refrigerators, washing machines, dishwashers, etc. Their specific energy consumption also dropped by an average of 11%; however, the stock of equipment increased by 13%, so that power consumption increased slightly for this group, too.
- Only in the area of industry has there been a real reduction in energy consumption. While the value of production remained at the same level from 1995 to 2003, the specific energy consumption per euro of added value fell by 11%, a 9% drop being due to a decline in end-use energy consumption.

The desire for increased comfort and convenience is the reason that new devices are brought onto the market. One example is the growing popularity of single-room air conditioners in Germany, for example, where home air conditioning has hitherto been virtually unknown; now, ever more people are buying them for the country's few very hot summer days. That causes a significant increase in demand for electric power.

These examples show that a substantial realization of the reduction potential of energy consumption cannot be achieved with technical measures for improved energy use alone, i.e., with more energy-efficient equipment. People's behavior is just as important. They will have to contribute to realizing the reduction potentials – by heating less space and travelling fewer kilometers, for example.

In our classification of possibilities for reducing energy consumption, we can say in conclusion that both the behavior-related and the organizational measures each have the potential for achieving a 10% overall savings in consumption, without any substantial losses in the standard of living. Greater savings than that will require investments. Reduction potentials through changes in behavior can be developed over short periods of time, if people want. On the other hand, technically-based energy efficiency increases are tied to the life spans of devices. They can therefore be realized only in time periods such as eight years for cars or home appliances, or even thirty years for buildings.

Energy savings and energy-efficiency improvements require millions of individual measures. Each is politically unspectacular, in and of itself. That is the reason why support for energy savings is less in the limelight in the political arena than the development of renewable energies.

15 Hydroelectric Power and Biomass

Nature uses one quarter of the energy that the sun shines onto the earth to evaporate water. The water reaches the earth again as rain or snow, feeds the rivers and thus enables the use of its kinetic energy to run generators which produce electric power. Water power has been used for mills and mechanical propulsion systems since the Middle Ages. Since the introduction of electricity, it has been a proven source of power. Today, that is its almost exclusive use.

By contrast, nature uses only 1% of the sunlight that shines onto the earth to build biomass by way of photosynthesis; it has a carbon content of about 50%. On the average worldwide, about twelve tons of dry biomass grow per hectare forest or farmland every year; one hectare is 100 m × 100 meters, or about 2½ acres. Biomass has also been used by humankind since time immemorial, both in the food chain and, in the form of firewood, as an energy source. Now, modern processes also make it possible to gasify all sorts of biomass to produce marketable energy sources, or else to liquefy it as storable energy. In these forms, it can be used in transportation. It is worthwhile to have a closer look at these two options.

15.1 Hydroelectric Power

Today, water power is used almost exclusively to generate electric power. The kinetic energy of the water drives turbines, which in turn supply a generator with mechanical energy; this produces electricity. Ultimately what is being used is the potential energy resulting from the difference in altitude of the water, which is due to the fact that it has rained on higher areas, or snowed in the mountains and then thawed. Under these circumstances, hydroelectric power systems can supply a dependable amount of electrical output, i.e. at least the minimum quantity of hydroelectric power is foreseeable, so that hydroelectric power is a reliable energy source for the supply of consumers. The technical term for a hydroelectric-power system on a river is a "run-of-river" power station.

Run-of-river power systems are fairly expensive in terms of investment costs. Large masses of earth must be moved, and it is necessary to build large concrete structures. In terms of their building costs and their output, these systems are four to eight times as expensive as hard-coal power stations. On the other hand, hydroelectric power stations have the advantage of very long life spans and low business expenses. They are therefore among the more economical power-generating systems, in the long run.

A second way to use water power is in the form of pump-storage plants. In this case, the water is first collected in a reservoir located at a high altitude, from the creeks and rivers in a relatively large catchment area around the reservoir. Often, for conservation reasons, not all the water available in these watercourses is brought to the reservoir, but only about 80%. The reservoir is built for two different reasons. First, it serves to store the potential energy of the water, which can be taken from the basin and fed to a power station at a lower level at any time. That makes it possible, for example, to use the water from the spring thaw to generate power in the fall. Second, the reservoir has the task of meeting peak demands for electric power which may appear at short notice. Industrial plants and households do not need the same amount of electricity around the clock. Plants and equipment are turned off at night, while cooking stoves are needed around noontime, and when people come home from work in the evening; at that time, too, washing machines and dryers are loaded and TV sets switched on. Hence, there is additional need for consumption of electricity at certain times of the day, so that the power stations must provide more electrical output then. Such peaks are extremely noticeable during breaks in major sporting events. As long as the fans are watching the game, the apartments are dark and most of the electrical equipment is turned off. Then, at the beginning of halftime, the lights are switched on in the living room, in the refrigerators as the doors open, and in the bathrooms as the toilets are used. This can happens at the same time in up to 20 million apartments throughout Germany, so that the demand for electric power shoots up in seconds. Pump-storage hydropower plants are there to provide the technical solution – additional power, fast. The valve in front of the turbine is opened, and within two minutes, the turbine is turning and the generator is producing power. Other possibilities for producing electric power quickly are gas turbines, which are familiar on airplanes, for example. They too can start fast and help meet such demand peaks.

Where there is little natural water available to draw on, a different kind of pump-storage plant is used. Here, two reservoirs are built, one in the valley and one on the mountain, and the water in them is used to generate electricity. If a lot of electric power is needed, water from the upper basin is allowed to flow down to the lower one. If, on the other hand, little is needed, for example at night, power is taken from the grid to pump the water up again. Large pump-storage plants which operate in this way include the large system at Vianden, Luxemburg, and the most modern pump-storage plant worldwide in Goldisthal, Thuringia.

A look at the operational chart of these large systems shows busy activity during a day. Over the course of twenty-four hours, it is not at all unlikely that power will be produced fifty times and then water pumped back up again fifty times. In addition to the plants' task described above of meeting demand peaks, there is also a second purpose to some of these facilities. For physical reasons, the electrical consumer actually needs not only electrical energy; he or she also needs it in two forms: first, the effective power, such as that which produces the heat for a stove, and driving power, such as what drives a power drill. In order for the power drill to turn, magnetic fields must be built up and then turned off again, i.e., reactive power has to be available. The generator must provide this, too, in the quantity required by the consumer at all times. Pump-storage plants are very frequently used for this, because they can react fast.

While a run-of-river power station is a real energy producer, a pump-storage plant which only serves to meet demand peaks, with no inflow into the upper reservoir, is actually an energy consumer, for power is used to pump the water up the mountain, possibly from coal-fired power stations. The pumps cannot operate without loss, nor is the electrical propulsion of the pumps or the pipes loss-free. If the water runs down the mountain again, it suffers loss of energy due to friction in the pipes. After that, it drives the turbine, which is also not quite loss-free, which drives the generator, which is not loss-free either. Of every 100 kWh of electrical output taken from the grid to power the pump, 20 kWh will be converted to technically useless heat, according to the laws of physics, and ultimately, at a different time of day, the remaining 80 kWh can, in modern systems, be fed by the generator into the grid as electric power.

With today's state of the art, pump-storage plants are the only way to store large quantities of electrical energy using the detour of potential energy. No other storage medium can do so on such a scale. This is reason why we are discussing pump-storage plants in the context of the use of renewable energy sources. On the one hand, it would be possible to pump the water into the upper basin with the help of electric power from wind energy systems. That would permit a decoupling of the wind-power supply from the demand side. On the other, more pump-storage plants could be built to be used if, due to major fluctuations of the wind, the output of conventional power stations had to be increased or reduced very rapidly. However, it must be taken into account that good wind sites are often far away from the low mountain ranges in which pump-storage plants can best be built.

Some 16% of the electric power produced worldwide is from hydroelectric facilities. In some countries, it is the most important source of electricity. Norway gets 99% of its electric power from water, Brazil 84% and Canada 58%. In Germany, hydroelectric facilities provide little more than 4% of electricity consumption. Moreover, there is little scope for further development of this source in Germany; on the other hand, worldwide hydroelectric-power capacities are far from being exhausted yet. This does not necessarily mean the construction of new hydroelectric power systems, but largely the modernization and expansion of existing systems. Rebuilding the hydroelectric power station at Rheinfelden on the upper Rhine for example will be able to quadruple output from 26 MW to 100 MW. During the 1990s, many small hydroelectric power stations which had previously been shut down were reactivated; hence, almost 6800 small hydroelectric power systems – "small" means less than 1 MW – are in operation in Germany. However, by far the major share of the 4% of Germany's electricity provided by hydroelectric power comes not from these privately operated systems, but from 120 larger systems – i.e., those producing more than 1 MW – located on the larger rivers and operated by the electricity companies. Due to their size and the greater availability of water, they provide 80% of the annual production of hydroelectric power.

The "large" European hydroelectric power stations are, by worldwide standards, small. An electricity generating unit in a modern hard-coal-fired power station has an output of 700 MW; theoretically, it should be able to meet the requirements of a city of about 700,000 inhabitants. The storage power stations Malta and Kaprun in Austria are in this output range. The largest run-of-river hydroelectric power station in Germany however, has an output of only about 20% of this level. This is simply due to the available water supply and the usable height difference. Rivers like the upper Rhine are therefore covered with a cascade of power stations, one after the other. On the Moselle and other rivers, there are locks, so that the ships can overcome the difference in altitude of the dammed water; some rivers have only been made navigable in the first place by this means.

Measured in European terms however, truly gigantic power stations have been built in other parts of the world. The world's biggest storage power stations are the Three Gorges Dam project in China, the Itaipu Dam in South America, on the border between Brazil and Paraguay, and several dams in Siberia, such as at Bratsk. These huge dams provide electrical outputs fifteen times as great as those of a single coal-fired power station. The output from in Itaipu would suffice to supply all of Belgium and Luxemburg with electrical power. Hydroelectric power systems of this order of magnitude have considerable impacts on nature and also on the living space of people. According to press releases, one million people have been resettled for the Three Gorges Dam project in China. Such large quantities of stored water are also a potential threat in case of a break in the dam wall; vast areas would be inundated and many people endangered. Renewable energies used locally on such a scale are no longer environmentally neutral. Even run-of-river power stations such as those built in Germany require a number of ecological compensation measures. These include near-natural fish stairways and spawning waters, or the creation of flood-plain forests.

Hydroelectric power provides a further worldwide potential for the generation of electricity. It has the advantage that it does not involve the consumption of additional resources – other than land – and does not emit air pollutants or greenhouse gasses. Water power is storable, for run-of-river power stations ensure a predictable minimum quantity of water and hence hydroelectric power is easy to tie into the power grid, which is subject to fluctuations caused by changing consumer demand.

15.2 Biomass

The significance of wood for the supply of rural areas in developing countries has already been discussed above (page 63); it will therefore not be addressed here. Rather, let us examine the potentials which biomass has as part of the energy supply mix in the industrial and emerging-market countries. In addition to wood, other biomasses sources also exist (Figure 14), including agricultural wastes, garbage, and sewage gas from sanitary landfills. Various processes can be used to turn the various biomass components into gas, alcohol or oil products.

Biomass therefore has the capacity to cover various areas of

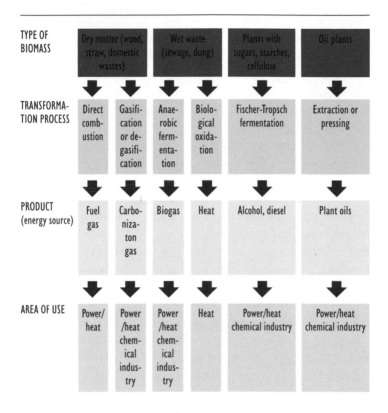

Figure 14 Forms of biomass, and their transformation to various energy sources

application in the energy supply mix. The gas can for example be used as fuel for heating farmsteads or nearby buildings. With chemical conditioning – biogas consists of 50–70% methane, 30–40% carbon dioxide, and traces of hydrogen sulfide, hydrogen, nitrogen and carbon monoxide – it can also be fed as an additional component into the existing natural-gas supply system. Alcohols can be used as raw materials for the chemical industry, but can also be used in special vehicle fleets in the traffic sector. During the 1980s for example, Brazil launched a large-scale ethanol program, due to the oil-price rise; the ethanol was obtained from the sugar cane from plantations. At its peak over 20 million vehicles in Brazil ran on ethanol. However, with falling world market prices of oil, the number of vehicles operated by ethanol dropped again toward the turn of the millennium. The physical and chemical transformation processes require a high level of know-how and efficient process control. The research and development requirement in this area has also not yet been met. The use of biomass is not environmentally neutral. In particular, air pollutants can be produced, which, like the air pollutants from the combustion of coal and oil, must be minimized by end-of-pipe technologies.

An essential cost item involved with the use of biomass is the collection of the biomass for use in the transformation facility. Gathering wood or agricultural scraps is labor-intensive, and often involves long distances; ultimately it is expensive. Therefore, not every tree lying in the woods can be burned in a wood-fired power plant. It would be too expensive, measured in terms of conditions in an industrialized country, moreover, it is also necessary for ecological reasons to allow a certain quantity of biomass to rot in the forest.

Thorough examinations undertaken by various institutions unanimously certify the following potentials for biomass: Europe-wide, the available biomass accounts for about 10% of the present total primary energy requirement.

To put the order of magnitude of these figures into perspective, here are some examples: If it were theoretically possible to use half of the available quantity of biomass in Germany for the generation of electricity, it could cover about 10% of today's electric-power consumption. That is double the potential for hydroelectric power. If the other half of this available biomass in Germany could then be used for fuel production, about 7 million tons of gasoline and/or diesel could be replaced. These would equal 12% of today's fuel consumption, as noted above. One decisive advantage of biomass use is comparable to that of the use of hydroelectric power: the energy can be easily integrated into the existing energy supply mix, in this case because it is storable.

One option of biomass use is to set up energy plantations on fallow agricultural land. Fast-growing plants, such as *miscanthus*, a kind of reed grass also known as "E-grass" (a name that originally stood for "elephant grass," which is actually a different plant, but now suggests "energy grass," due to its increasing use for biomass), or poor-quality grain types can be used as energy raw materials. Tests have shown that seventeen tons of E-grass can be reaped per hectare per year. After deduction of the energy needed for cultivation and harvesting, that represents a net yield with as much energy as is provided by 5600 liters of fuel oil. The yield from the grain, however, is only about two thirds of that from E-grass; only a little over eleven tons can be reaped per hectare, for a fuel oil equivalent of about 3000 liters.

In the case of the cultivation of grain, a family that today heats its home with oil and of course drives a car with oil products, would need approximately one hectare to substitute its annual oil consumption in this manner. With 20 million families in Germany, 200,000 sq. km. of area, or 56% of the entire territory of Germany would theoretically be required. This figure shows that the use of biomass is greatly limited. It would also have to be taken into account that this would be a monoculture which would on the one hand be very sensitive to pests, and on the other would need a high input of artificial fertilizer to maintain the agricultural productivity of the soil. Neither factor can be viewed uncritically from an environmental point of view.

Another example demonstrates the energy density of biomass: it is the answer to the question as to how many cows a household would statistically need to meet its energy needs for heating and driving with biogas. A cubic meter of biogas has approximately the energy contents of 0.6 liters of fuel oil, so that about 5000 cu. m. of biogas would be needed. A cow produces about 10 to 20 kg of dung per day, which would yield 1 to 2 cubic meters of biogas. In a year, a cow thus produces the energy equivalent of 330 liters of fuel oil, so that nine cows would be enough to the supply the household. The interested reader may now investigate how much pastureland would be needed to feed these nine cows for a year. The result will certainly be substantially greater than the amount needed for the cultivation of the grain in the first example. The reason is that a cow is a very bad "energy-conversion machine" – although it has a number of redeeming qualities.

Wood pellets have also won a secure place on the heat market. They can be blown from a delivery vehicle by compressed air into containers in your cellar. The heating system is fed automatically, and the ash only needs to be removed every few days. From the point of view of convenience, they are therefore just as suitable as oil or gas heating systems, particularly for use in multiple dwellings. Limited manufacturing capacities for the wood pellets have caused their price to increase.

In summary, the potential for available biomass in Central Europe is very probably within the range of 10 to 20% of the present energy consumption quantities. However, this is the theoretical potential, which cannot in all cases be economically developed, when compared with other energy sources. It is important on the cost side to keep the collection expenses of biomass as low as possible. Just as a great variety of different biomasses is available on the supply side, there is also a great variety of more or less mature technological processes to convert the biomass directly into heat or else into gas, alcohol or oil products.

16 Solar and Wind Energy

Other than hydroelectric power, solar and wind energy are the most widely used renewable energies worldwide. Solar energy can be converted into usable energy in different ways. On the one hand, the solar radiation can be absorbed by a thermal collector, which then heats a medium, such as water. On the other hand, the photons of which solar radiation is composed can be used to bring charged particles into motion and thus produce electric power in a semiconductor compound. This process is called "photovoltaics."

In the past, wind energy was used primarily in water pumps – we recall the slowly turning waterwheels in westerns, which pumped water into a tank to supply steam engines. Modern windmills, which drive generators to produce electric power, were developed later. Today, windmills are used worldwide almost solely to generate electric power. Let us take a closer look at these technologies for using renewable energies.

16.1 Solar Panels

Solar energy collectors are simple structures. Their task is to absorb the incident rays of the sun, and to use the energy to heat water. The simplest systems are in those areas of the world where high solar irradiation is present, such as the Mediterranean region, or India.

Tubes are attached to black sheets of metal, and water is passed through them to a tank. The metal sheet, called the absorber, converts the radiant energy into heat and passes it on to the water. The warm water can then be removed from the tank, and at the same time, cold water is supplied into the system to be heated again.

Unfortunately, such simple systems are not useful in our latitudes, because of the low solar irradiation; here, the black absorber must be replaced by a flat-plate collector. This is a box-shaped device in the middle of which the collector body is installed. Toward the back, it is provided with an insulating layer, so that heat losses are kept down. On the side facing the sun, one or two glass plates are placed in front of the collector. They make it possible for the system to operate more effectively, because less energy is lost by irradiation when the absorber body is heated. Theoretically, a maximum temperature of up to 120° can be achieved with these systems; in practice, however, the temperature is kept down to the level of the desired temperature of the warm water, so that the most energy-efficient operating temperature of the system is 60°C.

Although it sounds so simple in principle, it is all the more ingenious in its technical realization. The absorber body and the glass tops are not of simple materials, but are selectively coated so that the absorber can absorb as high a proportion as possible of the spectrum of visible light. On the other hand, the coating helps ensure that radiation losses in the infrared range are not too great, which would reduce the degree of effectiveness of the system. Therefore, an additional selective coating ensures that less is emitted in this spectral range. The same applies to the glass plates: they are supposed to let the incident sunlight in and reflect as little of it as possible back, and ensure that the infrared radiation reflected by the absorber is reflected back again in the direction of the absorber.

All this is state-of-the-art now, and it makes the collectors technically demanding products, but it also costs money to produce. If all you want to do is heat water for the swimming pool in your yard, very simple systems will suffice, even at our latitudes. Unfortunately, the radiation availability throughout the year is not such that it would be possible to meet our hot-water requirements with solar collectors year-round. Systems with the cost side optimized, for example for a four-person household in a detached home, have a collector area of about 6 sq. m. and a tank with around 300 liters of water content, and can produce enough heat for approximately half our annual hot-water needs. The remaining heat must be obtained via a conventional heat system, either a boiler or else an additional electric heater. This system is sold on the market for about €5000, including assembly. Assuming a life span of twenty years, a private individual can deduct it at a rate of €250 per year. A CFO could add the lost interest, since he could have put the money in the bank instead of investing it in a solar system. At the same time, there are savings of about 200 cu. m. of natural gas or 200 liters of fuel oil per year, since the solar energy heats the water. Obviously, this system will not yet amortize itself at the energy price of 90 cents per liter of oil, which prevailed in mid-2008. Nevertheless, some one million solar-heating systems have been installed in Germany alone. A good measure of idealism, and also a government subsidy for this new technology, are the reasons for this market situation.

16.2 Solar Power Stations

That part of solar radiation which reaches the earth as parallel radiation can be concentrated with the aid of mirrors. It produces higher temperatures, and is used in sun-rich areas with high shares of direct radiation. Nine solar farm systems were built in California between 1984 and 1991, large fields of mirrors with parabolic troughs. An absorber tube is placed at the parabolic focus, where the radiation is concentrated. A thermo-oil flows through the absorber tube and is heated to a temperature of 400°C. These temperatures are enough to vaporize water in a boiler and thus to drive a conventional steam circuit for generating electricity. More than 15% of the incident solar energy can be converted into electricity in this way.

The remaining energy is either lost at the mirror or else cannot be turned into electricity due to the way the laws of physics apply in a steam circuit – the so-called "Carnot limitations." The systems in California were built commercially and have been operated commercially to this day. They produce electric power during the day, and must guarantee to deliver the quantities agreed upon. They are therefore equipped with a storage system in the form of storage tanks for the hot oil, or else an additional gas-fired burner. Given good local irradiation conditions, however, this backup system has to produce less than 15% of the total electricity. Some 350 MW, equal to about half the output of a generator in a modern hard-coal-fired power station, have been installed southeast of Los Angeles. Dropping gas prices and the absence of tax depreciation possibilities were the reason that during the 1990s, this technology was no longer economically competitive, and further development ceased. Not until 2005 was project work initiated again for the construction of another system. In 2007, an additional plant was brought online in Boulder City, Nevada, and in 2008 a plant was opened in Spain; two more facilities are under construction there.

Another interesting design with the same goal is the solar-tower system, of which a few test and prototype systems exist in the USA, France, Japan, in Italy, Russia, and at the European Test Center for Solar Energy Applications in Almeria, Spain. Not all these pilot plants are still in operation. With this technology, flat, so-called heliostatic mirrors are set up around a 50 to 100 meter high tower. They track the position of the sun, and the incident solar energy is reflected exactly onto the tip of the tower, and concentrated on the receiver there, which is in effect a heat exchanger. It passes the energy to a cooling medium, using air, sodium or water, depending on the system. Steam is then produced via another heat exchanger, which then operates a conventional steam-power station to produce electric power. The advantage of this technology over the solar farm system is that higher temperatures can be provided for the steam circuit, which increases the energy efficiency. To date, however, this technology has not gotten beyond the prototype stage. On the one hand, two new installations are being built in Spain; on the other, it also has to compete with the solar-farm technology, which has already been in use for over fifteen years.

The stimulus to build solar technology for power generation in California at that time was that additional power-station capacities were needed to meet the high daytime demand in summer for air conditioners. There was thus a good match between solar supply and the demand for power. This is not the case in Central Europe. The greatest demand for electricity here is in the winter months, when the availability of solar energy is generally less than during the summer. If solar systems are tied into the conventional power grid, the same problem would arise as in the case of wind energy: fluctuating supply is the reason that the power supplied by the facility is not a reliable energy supply; it may not be available when it is needed. Thus, while oil, coal or gas can be saved with this technology, it cannot make the construction of additional power stations unnecessary, since they will have to jump in in case of need. This has made the inclusion of solar power stations in the electrical-energy supply mix so much more difficult on the cost side that it has not taken place to this day.

16.3 Photovoltaics

The photovoltaic effect is the creation of an electric current in a solid as a result of the absorption of light – it was discovered almost 170 years ago. Photovoltaic cells consist of two extremely thin semiconductor layers of no more than 0.3 mm thickness altogether (Figure 15). These are differently "contaminated" with atoms of various other elements: in one layer, the so-called p-type layer, this causes a linkage to be free which can be occupied by an electron; in the other layer, the n-type layer, there is an extra electron which is not used for the linkage between the silicon atoms. It can be released with little additional energy, and then moves freely. As a result, an electrical field builds up in the semiconductor at the interface between the two layers, which ensures that the electrons which have been rendered energetically freely mobile by the incident sunlight now move outward through the electrical circuit. That makes it possible to produce electrical energy with the help of the energy of incident light. The fascinating thing about photovoltaics facilities is that they have no moving parts, make no noise, and are actually not subject to any wear at all.

The preferred material is silicon in various forms: as high-quality monocrystalline silicon, as multicrystalline silicon, or as amorphous silicon. Other semiconductor compounds are possible, in addition to silicon, including gallium arsenide (GAs), copper indium diselenite (CIS), and some others; some have already secured their share of the market.

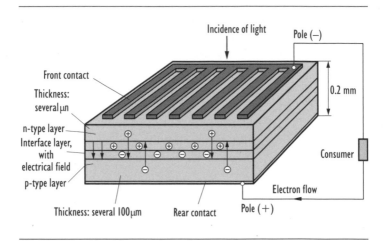

Figure 15 Schematic design of a silicon photovoltaic cell for solar-power generation

However, these photovoltaics modules are a little thicker and heavier than one would expect considering the thickness of the silicon layers of only 0.3 mm. They have to be held in a fixed shape, the electrical energy is tapped by means of contact plates and fingers, and ultimately, the whole thing must be protected by being embedded mechanically between glass plates. Another product is photovoltaics mats, also based on amorphous silicon, which have a somewhat thicker synthetic material on the back and are protected mechanically on the front by a thin permeable plastic layer. The technological development is very far advanced, and is in effect a mature system, but it is far from its goal as yet.

Well functioning photovoltaics facilities based on monocrystalline silicon can turn 15% of the sunlight into electrical energy. At noon on a warm summer day, the incident solar energy output amounts to about 1100 watts of thermal energy per square meter.

Thus, this solar cell produces 165 watts of electrical output, enough to power three light bulbs. Over the course of a year, 1000 kWh of thermal solar energy per square meter of horizontal surface can be generated, for an output of 150 kWh. A household with a medium-level stock of equipment uses more than 4000 kWh of electricity per year. To meet this need with a photovoltaics facility alone, 27 sq. m. of active photovoltaic surface would need to be installed – say 30 sq. m., including the area needed for the frames. However, that household could not cut itself off from the power grid, for the production of photovoltaic power is dependent exclusively on solar irradiation and the consumption of electric power in the household is subject to a different set of factors. The surface area required for solar panels is not an important factor, since experience has shown that there is almost always enough space available to set up a photovoltaic system. Therefore, a photovoltaics facility which operates with a considerably lower degree of efficiency than the 15% just described for a monocrystalline silicon panel can certainly be advantageous; it ultimately depends on the cost-benefit ratio. Amorphous silicon can be produced more cheaply than monocrystalline silicon, but yields less electrical energy from the incident light; still, it can be a good alternative in cost-benefit terms.

Photovoltaics alone cannot guarantee the electric-power supply of a consumer; storage systems for the electricity or a secondary power-supply system must be available. Photovoltaics is excellently suited to operate one or two lamps in a houses, or to power a telecommunications systems, a refrigerator or a TV set in developing countries. Remember that 1.6 billion people worldwide are still not connected to a power grid. For these purposes, batteries such as those we use in cars are possible storage systems for electrical energy.

Photovoltaic power generation is very expensive in comparison

with the power we get "from the wall." Large photovoltaic facilities in the megawatt range, in which the economies of scale are
already exhausted, still produce power at a cost of 35 ct per kWh,
while the electric power from our outlets costs us just over 18 ct
per kWh. The calculation is different, however, for the areas of
application in developing countries mentioned above. Here, the
power which solar panels replace may come from a diesel-driven
generator. Including the cost of transportation, the price for a
liter of diesel would be about €1.50, and it could generate 3 to
4 kWh of electricity; hence, the cost would be within the same
range as that of photovoltaic power, or even higher. Under such
conditions, photovoltaics makes economic sense. Since the utility
of photovoltaics often depends on the storage question, it is primarily suitable for systems for which small outputs are needed,
such as for powering television sets, refrigerators or lamps.

Government financial support measures for the development
of photovoltaics in various countries have caused the installation
of photovoltaic panels worldwide to rise continuously. In 2007,
it amounted to 3.8 gigawatts (GW) of electrical output, a figure
that is difficult to conceptualize, so that we might better view it
in a comparison: A nuclear power plant has an electrical output
of 1.3 GW; on the coldest day of the year, Germany maintains
80 GW of power-station output to assure its power supply; and
total worldwide installed power station output amounts to about
3600 GW. Let us not forget, however, that the conditions which
would provide such maximum photovoltaic output occur at the
latitude of Germany only for a few hours a year. Despite all the
successes of recent years, photovoltaics is therefore still far from
being a "major player" in economic terms in the electric-power
generation picture. The share of the power generation of photovoltaic systems installed in Germany is about one percent. The
keys to opening the photovoltaics option as a major energy-

supply factor is in the industrialized countries, where the expense of producing photovoltaics facilities has to be brought down through further technological advances. The peripheral parts of the system largely involve known technology, so that the cost reduction potential is in the photovoltaics component itself. Government support for photovoltaics makes sense in terms of acceleration of technological developments and opening up its potential, as well as in order to guarantee sufficient markets to maintain a critical industrial capacity. The photovoltaics industry could then earn its money in the niche markets in which it is already competitive today.

The introduction of photovoltaics at a scale significant for the energy industry is not possible at the present cost level. One example will serve to show the scope of financial support which that would require. Say we wanted to produce 10% of Germany's electric power from photovoltaics. It would be necessary, given German irradiation conditions, to install a photovoltaic output capacity of 50 GW, or an amount equal to approximately half the capacity of all power stations existing in Germany in 2007. If that large number sounds surprising, remember that under German conditions, a photovoltaics facility with one kW of rated output can only produce a little less than 1000 kWh of electricity a year – half what it could deliver in sunny areas elsewhere in the world. It could be assumed that, given this large number of systems, the investment costs would drop considerably – and the electricity-generation costs along with them. We have noted that photovoltaic power now costs 35 cents per kWh; let us assume that we could force that down to only 25 cents per kWh: we would then still have to bridge a gap of about 20 cents per kWh compared with today's production expenses in new power stations. Projected onto a 10% share of electric-power generation, that would represent a total of €10 billion per year in additional investment funding for photovoltaics that would have to be raised. One might correctly object at this point, that in terms of the kilowatt hour, that would only be a matter of a few cents. But the appropriate question in this situation is a different one: Could not the same desired environmental and resource-saving effect be achieved with less money – for instance, by investing it in energy-saving measures? That would permit environmental goals in the form of CO_2 reductions to be achieved more cheaply than by such an expansion of photovoltaics.

The above examples and arguments apply to conditions in the first decade of the 21st century. They may no longer apply in twenty or thirty years. As the examples show, the key to the introduction of photovoltaics at a scale relevant to the energy economy is not a price increase for fossil fuels, since, while that might narrow the gap, it would not close it. The key is the reduction of the costs of photovoltaics production. There are a number of approaches which would make such a reduction realistic over the course of the next few decades.

16.4 Wind Power

Western Europe is located in a zone of a good supply of wind energy, viewed on a world scale. The kinetic energy of the wind is a function of the wind speed to the third power. This formula means, for example, that the energy content of the wind increases eight-fold if the wind speed doubles. For this reason the best wind sites can be found along the coast or, further inland, at high locations. Under otherwise equal conditions, the difference in wind supply can cause the electric-power yields of a good coastal site and a mediocre inland site to differ by 25%. There are also differences of up to 20% in wind energy supply between one year and another. In the energy industry, the term "duration time" has been introduced to allow an easy calculation of the possible generation of electric power per year, based on the output of a single facility or of a wind park. It is calculated by dividing the electric-power output produced in a year by the maximum output of the wind-energy facility. The initial assumption is that the facility runs constantly at its maximum output from the first hour of the year on. The number of hours it would theoretically have to operate per year in order to produce the electric power which it feeds into the grid, is called the "duration time," measured in hours. For good sites on the North Sea coast, 2200 hours per year have been ascertained. Poor sites in the interior have scored only 1600 hours per year. The German average duration time is about 1900 hours per year. Figure 16 contains measurements recorded at a wind park during the months from January through March and from July through September 1997. These results show that there were considerable differences in wind supply, and hence in electric-power generation. The wind changes its output rapidly, and can vary between zero and maximum output. It is also interesting that the output for which the wind energy system has been designed is seldom achieved. As was even obvious visually, the wind park could, on average, be operated at only 30% of its output capacity during the three winter months measured, and at an even lower rate than that during the three summer months.

Wind energy requires additional power stations of the same scale of output as that of the wind system itself. Only about 5% of the overall wind output in Germany is considered secure output, i.e. only 5% of the installed wind system output does not need to be covered by other power stations. Thus, like solar energy, wind energy also saves coal, oil and natural gas, but not new power stations, since backup power stations are needed

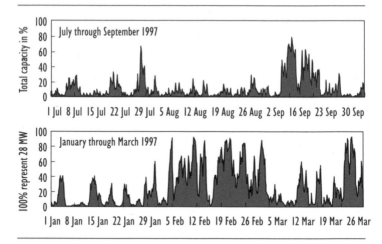

Figure 16 Time line of electric-power generation at a wind park with a total output of 28 MW

which can boost or cut their output very rapidly to compensate for differences between supply and demand. In practice, this problem is also frequently solved by having many power stations not running at their full output, so that all of them together provide the necessary backup output.

An inland wind-power facility with a maximum output of 2 MW produces 2000 kW for 1600 hours over the course of a year, or 3.2 million kWh of electricity – an impressive figure. A household in Germany equipped with a medium-level supply of electric devices uses more than 4000 kWh per year. Therefore, newspapers tell us that a windmill with that output would be able to supply 800 households with electricity – a large village, in other words. However, this is only statistically true, for if those 800 households had to depend only this windmill, they would face major supply problems. When no wind was blowing, they would have no electricity. If the wind supply were weak, they could not consume all the power they wished, but would have to ration it out among themselves in some way. Clearly, wind power is not a "stand-alone" source of electricity. However, the example also shows that the simplified news descriptions of the contribution of renewables to the energy-supply mix often do not do justice to the actual difficulties.

Storage systems for electricity are necessary. Unfortunately, no technical facilities are available to store electricity in large quantities for times in which the wind is not blowing. Battery storage or the flywheel energy-storage systems which are currently in development are at best suitable for ironing out fluctuations in time spans ranging from several minutes to several hours. Only by way of the detour through pump-storage plants can large quantities of electricity be indirectly stored in the form of "high-altitude water" over long periods of time. Current considerations include the ideal of compressed-air storage systems in addition to pump-storage plants: there are already two such systems in the world, one in the USA and one in Germany. Compressed air is forced into underground caverns, and can be released when required, so that its energy generates electricity. Another idea is to use the surplus power from wind-energy systems to produce hydrogen by electrolysis. The electricity would be used to split the water into hydrogen and oxygen. The hydrogen could then be stored, and could be used as fuel in transportation, or be turned back into electric power via a hydrogen fuel cell. Or it could be burned directly to heat buildings or produce process heat in industry. On the other hand, hydrogen is very expensive to store.

Wind energy has undergone an impressive development over the past two decades, both with regard to its technical development and with regard to its entry into the market. The electrical output of a single facility has risen continuously during this period. Most of the first major wind-energy facilities in California at the end of the 1970s still had outputs in the area of less than 100 kW; today, five-megawatt facilities (5000 kW) can be had.

At the end of 2007, wind energy systems with a total output of 94 gigawatts were installed worldwide, a capacity equal to that of all the power stations in Germany. Germany is the world leader in the use of wind energy; its 22,000 windmills account for one quarter of worldwide wind power capacity as of 2007, with the USA, Spain, India and China following on the list. The triumphal march of wind energy was made possible by various government financial support measures provided for by legislation. In Germany, in addition to research and development funding, the first facilities in the so-called 250-MW Program were subsidized either directly with investment grants or by means of a payment per kilowatt hour. Today, the payments made to the windmill operators are passed on to all power users under the provisions of the Renewable Energies Law, as explained above.

The rapid expansion of wind energy has largely exhausted the available capacities for the transmission of electricity in Germany's high-tension grid. Wind-power facilities must even be switched off at times, because the power they deliver exceeds the transportation capacities of the grid at certain points. Any further expansion of wind power will therefore necessitate expansion of the grid, with the appropriate investments. According to investigations, particularly the so-called Dena Grid Study (the Dena is the German Energy Agency, a semi-public company which promotes alternative energy sources), the existing length of the German integrated grid system will have to be extended by about 5% by 2015, with about 400 km upgraded and about 850 km newly built. The same situation exists in all other European countries which intend to expand wind power. These additional expenditures must be charged to the account of the large-scale industrial use of wind energy. Although the costs of the gen-eration of electricity from coal, oil and gas-fired power stations will increase in the future, since many of them will have to be replaced for reasons of age, wind power is still far from being economical as yet.

In Germany, the good onshore sites for wind-energy systems have largely already been used. Occasionally, there have been problems of acceptance which prevent the further expansion of wind power. The reasons include the visual effect of large wind parks, for example in tourist areas. This and the greater avail-ability of wind offshore, where the wind blows evenly and at a higher speed, so that the energy yield is twice as great as on land, are why the development of offshore wind parks has begun. Windmills have already been built on platforms just offshore in Sweden, Denmark and Great Britain. Technically speaking, these are systems developed for onshore operation. Conditions on the German coast require that future offshore wind parks lie further out to sea: in the North Sea, 50 to 80 km from the coast, and in the Baltic Sea, approximately in the middle of that sea. The depths of the water in these areas amount to thirty meters and more, which poses a major technological challenge for the building the foundations of the windmills. Technical availability must also be maintained, and a service team cannot be on the spot as fast as with an onshore system; yet a breakdown would mean a loss of power and hence economic loss. Moreover, the technical requirements at sea are different: the salt content of the air leads to greater material wear on all components of the wind-energy system, and high waves cause additional dynamic load to the structure. The wind-energy companies are meeting this challenge, and have already reached the point in the develop-ment of larger offshore wind-farm systems at which wind parks are now being built. Since the investment costs for the planned

194 Energy

wind parks, with sixty and more systems, are in the range of
€100 million, they will not be financeable by selling limited-
partnership shares, i.e., investment packages, as has been done
in the past. However, banks require not only sufficient technical maturity of the system, but also financial solidity and credit
standing on the part of the operator companies, to minimize the
risk. It is thus not surprising that large energy supply companies are participating in the development of offshore wind parks.
Whether these systems will become economically viable for the
operators, taking advantage of the financial support provided
under the Renewable Energies Law, is still an open question.
However, the policy signs seem to point toward a willingness
on the part of legislators to adapt the feed-in provisions to the
changed conditions – i.e., upward.

The further development of wind energy still promises great
potential worldwide. However, the integration of wind energy
into the grid is not easy. It requires stable grids, sufficient conventional power station capacities to replace the wind energy
at any time, and, all in all, high investment costs. Under the
conditions pertaining in Germany during the next decade, the
cost of electric-power generation with wind systems will be at
least twice as high as that using conventional energy sources.
On the other hand, the technical know-how of the manufactur-
ers has grown immensely, and is being increasingly turned into
export successes – that is an item on the credit side of the ledger.
By comparison with power generation using fossil fuels, wind
energy is more environmentally friendly. However, it cannot
alone guarantee a secure power supply. While this is theoretically
possible, it would require a major increase in storage systems –
either many more pump-storage plants, or else the electrolysis
of hydrogen, as described above. On the other hand, there is the
practical problem that there are not enough sites available for

pump-storage plants, that it would take decades to build all the facilities needed, that long transmission lines would be necessary from the wind-energy sites on the coast to the pump-storage plants in the mountains, and that a major grid expansion and the building costs for the storage systems would involve very high in the case of pump storage and higher still in the case of a hydrogen-based system. On the other hand, these statements are not an argument against such storage systems being used increasingly over the long term.

Realistically, we can assume that wind energy in Germany could grow from its present 7% share of power generation to at most 20% within the next two decades. Worldwide, the development of wind energy will also occur in similar dimensions wherever the wind availability is good. However, it is necessary to take unusual features into account. For example, some rural regions in India today with a good wind supply do not have a stable power grid yet. Many smaller companies produce their own power with the aid of diesel-operated generators. Here, wind power is already economically viable, in connection with these existing generators. The demand for wind systems is accordingly very great.

Energy Use Is an Ethical Question

17 Energy Supply – The Key Question

It may sound surprising at first that the question of energy supply and energy use is a moral one. One would rather expect that it would have to do with political, economic and technical issues, but not with inner values and basic philosophies of life.

The ethical dimension of the energy issue becomes clear if we consider that energy supply is a key question for the further social and cultural development of a growing human race, and even for the preservation of the basic conditions of life for the existing population of the world – be it an improved food supply, better sanitary and medical conditions, heating in winter or air conditioning in hot areas in summer: everything is connected to energy conversion and energy use. Even if the access to energy sources were not limited quantitatively and were accessible without political barriers for all countries of this world, there would still be another barrier: cost. Developing countries in particular have problems providing themselves with enough of the energy they need. Energy is traded as a commodity worldwide, for so-called "hard currency." The weak national currencies of African countries have no place on the world energy market. To get hard currency, these countries have to sell goods on the world market which other countries need or will buy, such as agricultural products, tourist attractions, or raw materials, such as ores or crude oil. With increasing oil prices on the world market, developing countries have limited possibilities for earning additional money through the export of additional goods. For the industrialized countries on the other hand, cost may be a factor economically, too, in terms of imported energy sources, but ultimately, industrialized countries can, by making efforts to increase exports, earn a part of their foreign exchange that they will need to pay the higher prices for energy elsewhere on the world market. Often, their manufactured goods go to the very countries from which they import their energy.

Keeping the price of energy on the world market low is therefore not only a matter of economic rationality, but also a question of morality. Increasing prices of energy reduce the standards of living in developing countries – to the extent that the manner in which their people live cannot even be described as a "standard" at all. On the other hand, low or falling energy prices would enable them to obtain the energy sources that they urgently need more easily on the world market.

The considerations discussed so far are rather related to current events. If we look further into the future, the question of the quantity of cheap, available energy resources arises. In particular, oil is, thanks to its good transportability, its good storability and its relatively simple manageability, *the* energy source for developing countries. In the long run, the industrialized countries will therefore have to consider from an ethical point of view whether they can reduce the use of that energy source which is best suited for developing countries.

Industrial nations have the advantage that they have a variety of technological possibilities at their disposal; the less developed nations, on the other hand, do not.

18 Choice of Energy Sources

The public discussion – particularly in the industrialized countries where it takes place on the basis of a high standard of living – is increasingly addressing the question as to which energy source we would like to use. It comes to a head in the discussion around nuclear energy and/or renewable energies. Germany has taken the political decision not to use nuclear energy as an energy source in the future any more, and on the other hand to tie wind energy into the electric-power structure to a considerably greater extent. Both of these are options which are not available to most developing countries in this way, for they are both, first of all, capital-intensive, and second, require a high level of technical knowledge for the construction and operation of the systems. Particularly the integration of renewable energies into the existing energy-supply structure is not always possible without problems. Wind energy provides a fluctuating electric-power supply, while consumers need the power in accordance with their lifestyle and needs – and that is true, too, in developing countries. Moreover, we are still far from a solution to the problems of energy storage – both economically and technically.

Ethical issues are a factor in a decision to use one energy source rather than another. The question as to the criteria upon which such decisions are to be based thus arises. Two frequently cited principles are that of an "existence worthy of human dignity" formulated in the UN Declaration of Human Rights of 1948, and that of "sustainability," defined by the Brundtland Commission. The first needs no further elucidation. The second, sustainability, is defined in terms of several different dimensions: social, economic and environmental. According to the social dimension, everybody should have the means necessary for a dignified human life, and the possibilities of future generations should not be restricted by our energy consumption today. The economic dimension demands that energy be available, reliably and at competitive prices. That ultimately means that consumers should be able to tap a quantity of useful energy any time they need it, or think they need it. The more highly developed an industrialized society is, the greater is its need for constantly available useful energy. In actual fact, what we really need is not the useful energy itself in its various forms, but rather energy as a service: mobility, lighting of a certain brightness, or rooms of a certain temperature. This service can be provided by means of various different quantities of useful energy, depending on the measure of energy efficiency. It is frequently said that energy is needed, and from the point of view of the consumer, that is certainly true. Yet the consumption of energy, like that of any other commodity in an industrialized society, ultimately consists of two components: actual need and active demand. Demand is managed for economic reasons through advertising and other motivation-promoting measures. The requirement to go to work creates a need. The desire "to go for a spin" in the car or to experience a feeling of freedom on a motorcycle on the weekend contributes to demand.

Based on this, we could formulate the requirement to bring demand back as close as possible to need. However, we can see in practice that this will be very difficult, because many things which give us pleasure, such as travel, ultimately involve energy consumption. Energy saving is not an issue in daily life.

All in all, the availability of useful energy has permitted an ever better lifestyle over the past decades, and, together with improved medical services, has also contributed to an increase in life expectancy. Therefore it is not surprising that the production of enough useful energy for the people is a key policy question in most developing countries. We can see in the emerging-market countries China and India that even these different cultures do not generate different demands or goals in the field of energy use than our societies in the USA or Europe do. It is therefore not justified to argue that due to different traditions, life-styles and philosophies of life, a lower energy requirement per capita than in the industrialized countries should be the goal in those countries.

If we break down the three dimensions of sustainability still further, so as to make them more manageable, we can define so-called compatibilities as criteria for evaluation: social compatibility, environmental compatibility and economic compatibility. This means that each measure to be taken must be brought into harmony with the existing political and social systems and their requirements. For example, environmental compatibility would mean having clean air and clean water, or agricultural land with as little acidification of the soil as possible. Stable climate and vegetation zones must also be seen as a prerequisite for the worldwide cultivation of crops.

However, there is no such thing as a completely emission-free energy supply or energy conversion system, or one with no effect on the economic and even the social system. For example, the construction of large dams provides electricity for the construction of economic and lifestyle prosperity, yet it consumes large areas and can permanently affect the basic living conditions of local people. Thus, within the actually non-controversial goal of the development of the energy supply, concrete conflicts of goals can arise. Newspaper reports about oil fields in African countries occupied or foreign experts kidnapped by the local people show the nature of these conflicts. They will have to be solved locally through dialogue and political compromise.

The answer to the question as to which particular energy sources and which technologies will best satisfy these general criteria requires a much more multifaceted approach. Here, individual energy sources and energy technologies are evaluated comparatively in extensive studies, according to established criteria. The EU Commission too has addressed the issue of criteria – called "indicators" – for the evaluation of particular energy sources from the general aspect of sustainability. The result is that none of the available energy options is completely free of technical, ecological, social and/or political risks. The various possibilities of energy supply bear different risks and different consequences, which make systematic comparisons difficult. The choice between them therefore involves great uncertainties. Beside the risk of impacting on the world's climate through the output of CO_2 and thus intruding massively on the cycles of nature and the food-chain, there are also the political risks of insufficient energy security of oil and gas, the technical risks which can potentially occur in connection with nuclear power, economic deficits in the use of renewable energies, and the still unresolved question of their storage.

The question is ultimately one of spreading the risk – both between the industrial and the developing countries and between present and future generations. Indisputably, developing countries are less able than industrialized countries to handle risk, regardless of its nature. A fair tradeoff is therefore necessary here, too, as it is in regard to an answer to the question of which energy sources are to be used and which are not. Which additional risks and consequences will for example arise if a given energy source, such as nuclear power, is not used? I will not attempt here to undertake an evaluation of nuclear power from an ethical point of view, as it would be beyond the scope and goal of this book. However, this consideration too demonstrates the ethical dimension of the energy issue.

19 The Time Frame

Another interesting question is that of how to deal with the time frame. We assess options and technologies according to today's criteria, but in doing so, we must ask ourselves which consequences our actions will have for future generations. It is frequently asserted that damage and disadvantages which will occur in the future should be assessed from our present point of view, according to the same standards as we assess the damage and the disadvantages we experience today. This assumption amounts to a principle of equality applied to the ethics of the future which is not applied in other areas of life, such as economics. In economics future effects are discounted, in other words, they are assessed as less important than those which take place today. Just as dynamic calculations are undertaken for every investment-accounting process, according to which income and expenditures are counted back with a discount factor to today's conditions, so that future payback flows are of less value with reference to today, so too must such a discounting appraisal be applied to the resource economy.

The aspect of the learning functions is also being discussed in this context. Just over the past fifty years, there has been considerable progress in the area of efficient energy use. Half a century ago, natural gas was not available on the world market yet. Can we therefore assume that the next generation will make no more technological progress which would have a positive effect in terms of energy consumption, or open up access to additional energy sources? Possibly, the next generation will succeed in developing nuclear fusion as such a source, and in making it politically acceptable, or in extracting natural-gas hydrates from the sea in an ecologically compatible manner. Would we be better off today, if the generation of our grandmothers and grandfathers had renounced coal, while we today greatly prefer to use hydrocarbons as an energy source, because of the many advantages they provide over coal?

The questions raised here show that there are no model solutions, nor will there be. However, they also show the necessity of addressing the ethical dimension of the energy question. At the Environmental Conference in Rio de Janeiro in 1992, it was for the first time possible in the policy arena to unite almost all the nations of this world at least verbally behind the concept of sustainability. The ensuing Kyoto process would certainly not have proceeded so rapidly, had there not been this preceding discussion over sustainability. The compensation mechanisms established in the Kyoto Protocol in the area of greenhouse gases provide the possibility for reducing the emissions of those gases, to the economic advantage of both the industrialized and the developing countries.

Ultimately, these compensation measures will be a first step in the direction of a worldwide dialogue in the area of energy, a good first step – albeit perhaps motivated economically – toward dealing with the fact that energy is also an ethical question.

On the Way to the Energy World of the Future

20 Modeling Games for Tomorrow

In view of a feared shortage of fossil energy sources, especially oil, several world energy scenarios which dealt with the shortage of resources were undertaken during the 1970s. It was necessary to show possible well calculated ways for a secure supply to meet energy demand. New scenarios cropped up at the end of the 1980s, in which the issue was less the question of the shortage of energy resources than that of an energy-supply system that could keep air-pollutant and greenhouse-gas emissions as low as possible. Now, however, the issue of energy security is once again playing an important role, alongside greenhouse-gas reduction. Such scenarios are being developed by large oil companies such as Shell, by scientific institutes, and by international organizations like the International Energy Agency in Paris, the European Commission and the Intergovernmental Panel on Climate Change.

20.1 Scenarios and Forecasts

An energy scenario is an assessment of the future development of energy consumption, as well as a structure of need and supply, under freely selected terms and specifications. It thus represents a simulation game of future events, an "if-then" calculation. Unlike an energy forecast, an energy scenario seeks not to predict as exactly as possible what will occur over the next ten years, for example, but rather to analyze and evaluate the various mathematical combinations, conclusions for boundary conditions and possibilities for future energy supply. For instance, calculations can be carried out which presuppose that emissions of greenhouses gasses will have declined by a given percentage by a given point in time. The energy scenario would then provide information as to which energy sources would have to be used at which scale, and possibly with which energy technologies. The next step, according to the simulation game, would then have to be a discussion between the experts of the different disciplines to determine which advantages and disadvantages these paths would have, and to what extent they would even be socially and politically feasible. Finally, the conclusions could be passed on to the decision-makers.

Those who develop scenarios, however, are no more free of the *Zeitgeist* in their assessments than anyone else. They too cannot reliably foresee all changes in the major boundary conditions, such as the development of the price of energy. Therefore it seems reasonable to redraft energy scenarios, or to adapt them to new boundary conditions at intervals of from five to ten years.

20.2 Worldwide Considerations

In this section, let us take a look at the conclusions for the expected course of worldwide primary-energy consumption and security, from five studies drafted over the last few years. The studies considered are:

1. EC [European Commission] (2003): *World Energy, Technology and Climate Policy Outlook*

2. EIA [Energy Information Administration] (2004):
   International Energy Outlook 2004
3. IEA [International Energy Agency] (2004): *World Energy
   Outlook 2004*
4. IPCC [Intergovernmental Panel on Climate Change] (2000):
   IPCC *Special Report – Emission Scenarios*
5. Shell (2001): *Energy Needs, Choices and Possibilities –
   Scenarios to 2050.*

Some of these studies describe several possible development
paths. They are each based on different fundamental assumptions
about the availability of conventional and renewable resources,
population growth, and economic growth. In addition, there are
differences in detail regarding assumptions of technical param-
eters, and the costs of energy systems. All in all, a broad range
of conceivable development possibilities is covered. The results
for worldwide primary energy requirement and CO_2 emissions
are shown in Figure 17. We should bear in mind that the studies
have different target years, ranging from 2025 through 2030 and
2050 to 2100. For purposes of comparison, the statistical values
for 2004 are shown.

The CO_2 emissions in the IPCC scenario are a predefined
target. The purpose of the scenario is to determine whether the
reduction in CO_2 emissions considered necessary can be achieved
on the energy-supply side, and how.

20.3 Expectations for the Future

All results show that none of these scenarios presupposes a reduction of world energy consumption, as compared with today's
value. On the contrary, the majority of the scenarios assume a

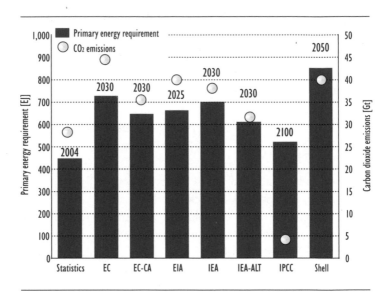

Figure 17 Results of various scenario observations for future world energy consumption and the output of carbon dioxide emissions (CO_2)

The year shown at the top of each bar is the final year considered in the respective study

considerable increase in primary energy consumption over the next twenty-five years. The proportional breakdown of energy sources which will cover that primary energy requirement is also informative. The shares for the individual energy sources which result from the different scenarios are as follows:

- Depending on the scenario, oil has a share of the primary energy supply of between 27% and 39% (today's value: 34%)
- The share of natural gas is between 21% and 28% (today: 21%)

–   Coal contributes between 8% and 28%, depending on the
    scenario (today: 24%)
–   Nuclear power accounts for between 4% and 7% (today:
    7%)
–   Renewable energies get between 8% and 33% (today: 14%).

Based on the expectations of the authors of these scenarios, we
can make the following statements about the energy supply of
the future:

–   No energy source is excluded
–   Fossil energy sources – oil, natural gas and coal – will still
    bear the main load of energy supply
–   Low-CO_2 and no-CO_2 energy sources like natural gas and
    renewable energies increase as a percentage of the total; coal
    declines, however
–   Oil and nuclear power remain approximately at today's
    level or drop a little, but these figures are percentages; since
    primary energy consumption increases absolutely, so do the
    required quantities of oil and the number of nuclear power
    plants.

It may seem surprising that no major modifications in the structure of the energy sources appear in the scenarios, but note that
the time horizon, 2030 in most scenarios, is relatively short.
Since the investments to be made in energy supply are high, the
technical life spans of the systems are long, so that the development of new energy sources would take several decades. Thus,
no extreme changes are to be expected over a period of a little
more than twenty years. An example from Germany shows what
this means in practice. Here, the scenarios expect investments
in electric-power generation alone in the range of between €90

billion and €120 billion through 2020. Shifting the shares of particular energy sources in the supply mix by even a few percent thus already means considerable change in practice.

In addition to a number of scenarios on worldwide energy requirements, there are also country-specific studies, such as for Germany. Unlike some of the world scenarios, these scenarios explicitly take into account the reduction specifications under the Kyoto Protocol, as well as the policy objectives of the government. For Germany, these factors include such measures as the planned increase in energy efficiency and the intended nuclear energy phase-out plan.

Unlike the world scenarios, the calculations for Germany arrive at a reduction of primary energy requirements of between 6 and 26% by 2020. The reasons for that include a slight drop in the population and the effect of measures for efficient energy use in all areas, such as power stations, and the improved insulation of buildings. However, these scenarios do not say anything about whether these measures are attainable politically.

21 Components of the Energy Mix

All ideas about the future, like those expressed in the scenarios described in the previous chapter, show that the future energy-supply mix will change not by leaps and bounds, but rather steadily. Investments in the technical life span of systems are too high to permit rapid breaks. Which direction the energy-supply picture in individual countries will move depends on many factors. Important boundary conditions include for example the development of the prices of energy, and access to energy and to technological developments. But the question of lifestyle and the social acceptance of particular energy sources and technologies is also important. Despite this uncertain background, "modules" can be defined, which will constitute the future energy supply picture. These include:

- the further development of power-station technology
- advanced heating systems which use the fossil energy sources coal, gas and oil
- improved engines with considerably lower fuel consumption
- cogeneration of power and heat production, both with larger systems for local and regional district-heat systems and small facilities for the supply of single buildings or building complexes
- renewable energies, particularly wind energy, biomass and the further development of hydroelectric power in some parts of the world, and

    – greatly improved energy efficiency in all areas of energy
       conversion and use.

These modules for the energy world of tomorrow are basically
already available technically, and in some cases also economically. Their contribution to future energy supply is foreseeable. In
addition, there is a variety of other technologies which can make
substantial contributions to increased energy efficiency or else to
the restructuring of energy supply. Their contribution cannot yet
be assessed, technically or economically. They include:

– hydrogen fuel cells and hydrogen technologies, for building a
    "hydrogen world"
– improved storage systems for electricity; they will help
    connect renewable energies to the existing power grids
– new insulation processes, such as vacuum insulation or
    transparent insulation; they will be able to provide savings
    even in cases for which today's technologies are not well
    suited
– expansion of efficient electrical grids across a continent;
    they provide a possibility for standardization of energy
    consumption, and
– if we expand our perspective to a time fifty years into the
    future, nuclear fusion, too, will have to be considered an
    additional option.

Which demands should we now make upon our modules and
technologies so that they will fit into the picture of future energy
supply? Let us examine this question in the following:

    The fossil energy sources and the systems needed for their
conversion will continue to be a substantial part of the energy-
supply picture all over the world. Technical design maturity

and reliability, and low investment costs will remain the central demands upon them. Moreover, high energy efficiency in energy conversion and low air-pollutant and greenhouse-gas emissions are needed. Today as in the future, the fossil energy sources coal, oil and natural gas will be used for generating electric power, for producing heat in large and small heating systems, and for satisfying the desire for mobility in the area of transportation.

21.1 Power Stations

Even in the past, the power-station sector stood out for the fact that due to the progress in materials science, ever higher temperatures and pressures could be achieved, which continuously increased the energy efficiency of plants. While at the end of the 1970s, new hard-coal plants still needed 280 grams of hard coal to produce one kilowatt-hour of electric power, nowadays just 180 grams is enough in the most modern systems. Combination power stations, in which a gas-turbine process and a steam-turbine process are coupled for the generation of electric power, have even much better energy efficiency than that. In the gas-turbine process, natural gas is burned. The flue gases, at 1300°C, flow to a gas turbine which drives a generator. Part of the energy of the hot exhaust fumes is converted into electricity, the remainder passes its energy on via a heat exchanger to a steam process, which also drives a generator and thus produces power via a steam turbine. It is also conceivable over the medium term that instead of the gas turbine, a high-temperature hydrogen fuel cell could be used. While at beginning of the 1990s, only 52% of the gas used could be converted into electric power, today's systems achieve 58%, and the design target is over 60%.

However, the special challenge in power station technology

will be how to pass as little CO_2 as possible on to the environment in the long run. We should not forget that we have already reduced the rise in greenhouse-gas emissions due to the considerable increase in the degree of transformation effectiveness. Nevertheless, the goal of developments is to completely remove CO_2 from the power-station process. In 2006, two companies announced plans to build pilot plants for this purpose. The separation of the CO_2 technically means that either it is washed from the flue gases, like sulfur dioxide, which is an expensive "end-of-pipe technology," or, with the so-called oxicoal process, that the combustion air is separated into its components, so that the flue gas is virtually pure CO_2. Finally, a third approach is that the coal is first gasified in a so-called pre-combustion process. All three processes will still need considerable development to make them technically mature.

Over the next fifteen years, approximately half of the power station parks in Central Europe will have to be replaced due to age; construction will have to start now. Power stations with CO_2 separation will be used on an industrial scale only in the generation after the upcoming one, i.e., in thirty to forty years. As good as this sounds, it also has its disadvantages. Climate protection and energy efficiency do not agree in this case. With CO_2 separation, the degree of effectiveness of a power station drops by 10%, depending on which process is used, due to the high energy consumption of this equipment – hence up to a third of the effectiveness achieved today will be lost again. This means that about one third more power station capacity must be built to produce the same amount of power – and it also means an increase in investment costs. As described in the chapter on greenhouse gas, the CO_2 emissions separated out can be pressed into empty natural-gas caverns.

21.2 Heat Production

The demands that will be made upon future heating systems will also be a maximum of energy efficiency and a minimum of air-pollutant emissions. Since the great majority of heating systems are in the small output range, such as boilers in residential buildings, the current state of the art does not allow the expensive CO_2 separation process to even be considered. That makes high energy efficiency all the more important; however, it has already been brought to near the limits of its technical possibilities. Heating-value equipment makes it possible to condense the steam in the exhaust fumes, created by the combustion of the hydrogen in oil and gas, to water. These devices reach degrees of effectiveness of 100% in practice. That sounds as if more heat energy can be gotten out of the device than has been put in at the outset in the form of natural gas – is it hence a "perpetual-motion machine?" Of course not. Rather, the degree of effectiveness, i.e., the ratio of the produced heat to the energy content of the natural gas used, is related to the heating value of the natural gas. However, this by definition does not take into account the condensation energy of the steam.

21.3 Transportation

We are all familiar with the transportation sector and its development, so we need not analyze it in detail here. The basic trend will be further improvement of the energy efficiency of engines. In the long term, today's consumption can be cut in half, according to estimates. We will have to consider, however, that in the past, increases in convenience and safety have obviated a considerable part of the technical gains in energy efficiency. Vehicles have gotten heavier and accelerate faster. That means greater energy consumption.

21.4 Nuclear Power

Nuclear power is used in many countries worldwide; some 440 nuclear power stations are in operation. The position of the industrial nations toward nuclear power varies widely, from political affirmation and the intention for further development, as in the USA and France, to the policy of phase-out, as in Germany and Sweden, or renunciation, as in Austria and Italy. A number of different technical series of nuclear-power stations are in operation worldwide, the largest number being the light-water reactors in western countries. In the past, they were technically designed with a "worst-case scenario" being a rupture of the cooling-water pipes. A melt-down of the core, as partially occurred during the accident in 1979 at the American Three-Mile Island nuclear power station in Harrisburg, Pa., was not the type of accident which the plant specifications demanded be fully controllable by means of the built-in technical security procedures. It was nevertheless shown that this accident in the Harrisburg power station could be controlled so well that no appreciable radioactivity was emitted into the environment. By contrast, the accident in Chernobyl, which was not a light-water reactor, had much more serious consequences for the population. New developments, like the European Pressure Reactor (EPR), which is currently being built in Finland and France, have a different safety philosophy. There, the meltdown is among the accidents that must be fully controlled technically, it is the "worst-case scenario." The graphite high-temperature reactor technology, developed in Germany and used in China and in South Africa, provides a high level of inherent safety for small reactors.

These aspects, the fact of CO_2-free power generation and the diversification of energy sources used, are the reason why many countries see nuclear power, too, as a future module in their energy supply systems.

Another possible option for future energy supply is nuclear fusion. Compared with nuclear fission, it provides the advantage that no more after-heat is generated after the fusion system is switched off, and no long-half-life radioactive isotopes are left over. Whether, unlike nuclear fission, it could therefore meet with broader acceptance in some countries, will not be discussed here. Its development will require much time and large, expensive pilot plants. They can no longer be financed by any single country. Therefore the next system (ITER) will be built by a worldwide team in Cadarache in the south of France. In terms of its physical development, nuclear fusion is still where fission was before 1938, when the first uranium isotope was split. First, it will have to be proven that the controlled fusion process can be achieved; then starts the long path to the development of a fusion power station, and making it technologically functional. All in all, fusion appears as an option which will not be able to contribute to the energy supply picture for at least another fifty years. It could have a really great potential then, however.

21.5 Cogeneration of Heat and Power

The cogeneration of heat and power, or CHP, has already been in use for about 100 years. It has now arrived at a high level of technical maturity, and provides energy savings of up to 15%, compared with the separate production of electric power and heat. It has the disadvantage that central heat-distribution grids are capital-intensive in construction, which makes district heat expensive, because of the long pipelines. In the past, district heat lost out in the contest with natural gas in many cities, because the providers of the gas were able, unlike those of the district-heat systems, to pay cities concession levies for the right of way on roads for building the pipelines. Another possibility is the application of the CHP principle in smaller systems, for example in hydrogen fuel cells or small engine-operated systems. They could supply single buildings or building complexes, and be connected via modern communication technology to a "virtual power station." A central control point could steer their operation and, for example, drive the systems preferentially at those times when the electricity is needed and more highly paid on the market.

21.6   Renewable Energies and Measures for Increased Energy Efficiency

All forms of renewable energies will continue to occupy a growing place in worldwide energy supply in the future. Which renewable energies are used will be different in each country. Their potentials, like those of efficiency measures, will not be discussed further here, since they have already been discussed in previous chapters in detail.

21.7   Hydrogen

The history of the energy industry and of energy technology is one of the development and market entry of ever new conversion technologies, with a considerable effect on the structure of energy supply. The hydrogen fuel cells and hydrogen technology, too, are widely viewed as having such a potential. Hydrogen is not an energy carrier that occurs in nature. Today, it is used as a raw material in the chemical industry, or in refineries to desulfurize, or "scrub," heating oil and diesel fuel. If this same amount of hydrogen were considered an energy source, it could supply 3 % of the world's primary energy requirements.

The major share of hydrogen used today is obtained by splitting natural gas. However, this method would not be suitable for a future hydrogen-energy economy, since natural gas can be used for the same purpose for which the hydrogen would then also be used. The production of hydrogen would be an energy-wasting detour, and would moreover be neither emission-free nor climate-neutral. Thus, the only way to go is electrolysis – the production of hydrogen by using electricity to split water. If that production is be carried out so as not to emit any greenhouse gasses, only electric power from nuclear power plants or from renewable energy sources is feasible. Hydrogen could be produced with the aid of hydroelectric power stations, photovoltaic plants, wind farms or solar-thermal power stations, such as those currently in use in California.

There have been strategies in the past for a future energy supply for Europe based on large-scale hydrogen production in the Sahara. This vision calls for covering a very large area of the Sahara with photovoltaic elements. Using the electric power thus generated, hydrogen would be produced from water by means of electrolysis, and would then be brought to Europe using pipelines and tankers, while part of the electric power could be transmitted via low-loss high-voltage direct-current cables (HVDC). Quantitatively, these concepts could certainly be realized, and the technical components for the creation of such an energy-supply system, too, are basically available today, although they would still have to be developed to maturity. However, calculations show that the costs per energy unit produced are considerably higher than the continued use of fossil-energy resources, even considering environmental-protection and greenhouse-gas-emission aspects. The Sahara vision also raises the question of the political accessibility to the energy carrier, since, as in the case of oil, large quantities of energy would be obtained from the Middle East. Nevertheless, these considerations show that if very high prices for energy are accepted – whatever consequences these may have for the economic prosperity of the countries involved – energy resources are still far from being exhausted.

21.8 Geothermal Energy

To complete the picture, let us mention a few additional potentials. Near-surface geothermal energy, i.e. from depths to approx. 60 meters, can be used with the aid of heat pumps. In 2008 for example, over 300,000 heat-pump systems are in operation for heating purposes in Germany; the technology is mature. Well designed heat-pump systems make it possible with an input of one kilowatt hour of electricity to obtain 3 to 4 kWh of heat from the soil to heat a building.

In addition, at some spots in the earth, existing hot-water stocks can be tapped into and used for heat supply for residential areas. Processes for the use of the normal temperature gradient of about thirty degrees of temperature difference per one thousand meters of depth are currently being developed, but are still in their infancy. This option could certainly be used over the long term for energy supply. It will provide more expensive heat than today's energy supply structure, however.

21.9 Storage

A central problem of any energy supply is the storage of energy. With the exception of the indirect storage of electricity via pump-storage plants, no storage system exist which can store electricity in large-scale quantities over an extended period of time. Although a large number of technical developments are in progress, no satisfactory solution is apparent as yet. Experiments include those for storage of electricity with supra-magnetic spools, with large flywheels, and with large battery systems. Heat can be stored in storage systems in the form of warm water, in the form of well insulated chemicals, and in gravel. What all these systems have in common is that they can provide only short-term storage.

If we could succeed in the future in finding new ways to store energy, especially heat, the entire energy-supply system could be restructured in many countries. We could tap our heat from a cogeneration system in tankers in winter, and dispense with expensive transportation networks. Super-sized solar systems could produce heat in summer for use during the transition periods and for winter. Wind systems could pass their electricity on to storage systems, to be fed into the grid when the consumer needed it. Unfortunately, we have to conclude these considerations with the realization that at present, we have no indication whether such storage technology will ever be found at all, so that we cannot foresee whether these dreams will ever be fulfilled.

21.10 Energy Transfer over Large Areas

Another interesting vision for the future of electrical-energy supply is the connection of entire continents using high-voltage direct-current grids, which make the long-distance transportation of electrical energy possible with acceptable losses. This is not possible with the alternating-current technology used today. Such an extensive grid, combined with the possibility of transporting electrical energy over long distances, could even out not only the climatic differences between, say, the warm climate of the Mediterranean and the colder temperatures in Scandinavia, but also the peaks caused by time differences in power consumption. When required, electricity from solar power stations in the Mediterranean area could be transported to Germany, or the other way around, wind power from Germany sent to the south. Although the technical possibility of HVDC exists today, the technical realization of such great energy transportation grids has not yet been planned concretely, both for economic and for political reasons. There are however single power lines of this type, for example between northern Germany and Norway.

21.11 Centralized vs. Decentralized

This discussion of technological developments makes no claim to being exhaustive. Nonetheless, the same basic conditions for inclusion in a future energy-supply system apply for the technologies not mentioned as for those discussed.

Often, differing fundamental positions are adopted in the energy discussion in connection with the future structure of energy supply, one position being that of a centralized energy-supply structure, the other that of a decentralized system. Large power stations which supply consumers by means of power-grid systems are considered components of a centralized energy supply structure. By contrast, hydrogen fuel cells, small-scale motor-driven cogeneration systems, wind-power systems and perhaps photovoltaic facilities at a variety of sites are seen as decentralized energy-supply systems. For heat supply, too, it is possible to juxtapose centralized and decentralized systems, albeit on a lesser scale. Here, a centralized energy-supply structure might involve a large-scale natural-gas system with lines leading to every house, or extensive networks of district-heat pipes in metropolitan areas, while decentralized systems might include wood-burning stoves, oil-fired central heating facilities or perhaps even geothermal energy systems. Clearly, existing power and heat supply systems tend strongly in the centralized direction.

There are pros and cons for each of these energy-supply structures. One "pro" for larger-scale systems is that they provide economies of scale, i.e. the reduction of the specific investment costs. Other "pro" arguments include the limitation of the reserve capacity to be maintained, and the increased supply safety in cases of system outages. Improved use of a variety of energy carriers, such as power generation from coal-fired plants in Germany's Ruhr Valley, or from hydroelectric power in the alpine countries or in Norway, is also possible with centralized supply structures. On the other hand, the supporters of decentralized energy-supply systems raise the vulnerability of large supply systems to natural disasters and terrorist attacks, the loss of energy in large distribution grids, and, last but not least, the issue of the political and economic concentration of control of the energy supply in large corporations.

The discussion of centralization or decentralization yields different visions of the future. From a purely quantitative point of view, it should be possible, on paper, to design an energy-supply system with exclusively centralized elements, and likewise one with exclusively decentralized elements. The question is, to what extent could such systems then be implemented in practice, considering the numerous limiting conditions of an economic, technological and political nature? Basically, the question arises as to whether the discussion is not being artificially determined by the definition of the concepts "centralized" and "decentralized." For instance, electric-power generation using a large number of fuel cells would without question be decentralized. However, since the fuel cells would have to be provided with natural gas, or perhaps in the future, with hydrogen, which would in turn have to be transported through large pipeline systems, the supply side would at least be a centralized energy technology. The heat production in oil-fired central heating systems, too, has a centralized component, if we consider the refineries or the large fields of oil wells.

The best way toward the future might be one which tries to combine as many components and technologies as possible into a future structure of energy supply. Such a system could react best to changing challenges; it would have both centralized and decentralized elements.

The Challenge of Energy — Using our Opportunities

22 The Facts

At the end of this book, it seems appropriate to summarize the facts and possibilities for action once again.

Access to energy is a prerequisite for dignified human life. We need energy in various forms in our everyday lives. Mechanical energy drives equipment and cars, thermal energy warms water and drives turbines, electrical energy gives us telecommunications, lighting and microwaves. Chemical energy is stored in coal, oil, gasoline and natural gas. The energy form which nature offers us is described as primary energy. It must be converted into a technically usable energy form. For this, we need power stations, refineries, gas pipelines, solar collectors, wind energy systems and nuclear power plants, along with enough transportation systems – pipelines, power lines and tankers – to ensure the infrastructure of energy supply. Consumers need energy services, i.e., warm rooms, light, information or process heat in industrial processes. Whether they are satisfied with plentiful or sparse useful energy depends, of course, on the laws of physics, and beyond that, on the technical level of the system, i.e., its energy efficiency, and in the case of heating buildings, also on their insulation.

The world population is growing continuously: 6.6 billion people were counted in the world in 2006. To date, world energy consumption has not followed the rapid increase in world population in the same measure. However, it has nevertheless increased steadily over the past fifty years. People use different amounts of energy. The major share of energy consumption is used to satisfy the needs of people in industrialized countries. About 20% of the people live in these countries, but they account for 50% of the world's primary energy consumption. However, the population is primarily growing in the developing and emerging-market countries, and not so much in the industrialized countries. Germany for example accounts for 1.3% of the world's population, and uses 3.5% of the world's primary energy production.

Not all forms of energy are the same. Each energy source is different in terms of ease of handling. The use of coal, oil and gas involves the emission of air pollutants and of the greenhouse gas carbon dioxide (CO_2). Flue-gas scrubbing processes are used to remove air pollutants from the combustion processes. This requires technical knowledge and additional investments, which make power generation about 20% more expensive. For consumers in developing countries, that is a considerable expense. The hydrocarbons petroleum and natural gas are being used up worldwide at a much faster rate than their share of energy reserves. Petroleum has the highest energetic density of all energy sources; it is storable and easy to handle. Therefore, 80% of mobility worldwide is fueled by petroleum products. It is also used for power generation in many countries. As a grid-bound energy source, natural gas is capital-intensive, as is electric power. It burns with lower air-pollutant emissions and lower CO_2 emission than other fossil energy sources.

The use of nuclear power presupposes high safety consciousness, a high technical security standard and the possibility of financing capital-intensive energy technologies. It is therefore primarily a technology for industrialized countries; for reasons of acceptability, however, not all of them use it.

Renewable energies are used in a wide variety of forms, and

with various technologies. Their use for heating water in sun rich areas is simple and very widespread. Technically more complex, and also more expensive, is power generation using wind-energy systems, solar-thermal power stations and particularly photovoltaics. Renewable energies are therefore not immediately accessible in developing countries for all. Wood as the fuel of the poor is the major energy supply in rural areas of the developing world. However, it is frequently used so extensively that it cannot regenerate itself sustainably any more. Desertification and karst formation are the result.

Energy is a commodity. The price of a particular energy source on the world markets, and also on most national markets, is determined by supply and demand, with consideration for the quality criteria of that energy source. The demand for the hydrocarbons petroleum and natural gas has increased considerably in the emerging-market countries of Asia and South America over the past few years. The development of new capacities and their political availability – affected, for instance, by wars in the Middle East – have not kept pace with this increase in the demand. The result is a considerable increase in the prices of oil and natural gas, which is a burden on the economies of the industrialized countries. Nevertheless, they still have the possibility of boosting their exports in order to earn the money they need to buy energy, including exports to the oil-exporting countries. Developing countries, on the other hand, have only very limited possibilities to obtain foreign exchange to buy energy. An increase in the prices of energy on the world markets means that they have to cut oil imports or other imports, and hence further reduced possibilities for developing their economies and securing an adequate standard of living for their peoples. It is therefore morally advisable to keep the price of energy low by reducing demand – i.e., by saving energy.

23 Renewable Energies – Our Hope for the Future

The existing energy supply picture worldwide, and in many industrialized countries, shows that more than 80% of overall energy consumption involves the use of coal, petroleum and natural gas. Hydroelectric power accounts for the largest share of renewable energies to date. The potentials of renewable energies have not yet been fully exploited worldwide. To do so, it will be necessary to overcome two considerable hurdles. One is that the energy provided by the sun arrives here at a low energy density. It must therefore be "collected" over large areas. For the use of solar energy, this requires greater investments than for the use of fossil energy sources, even considering all investments necessary for air-pollution control and the additional costs by CO_2 certificates. The second basic difficulty for the use of renewable energies is the fact that solar and wind energy fluctuate. Moreover, they are hard to store, since neither seasonal heat storage of sufficient quality nor storage for large quantities of electrical energy are technically available.

A central question of future energy supply, and thus also a central question of the further energy research and technical development, is that of storage. Solar and wind energy replace fossil and nuclear energy sources. However, they cannot replace conventional power stations or heat production systems to any considerable degree. They need conventional backup systems, which thus make the use of renewable energies additionally more expensive. The price for hard coal would have to triple, for example, for the use of wind power to become competitive from a strictly business-management point of view. The use of sunlight for electric-power generation by means of photovoltaics cannot become competitive by means of price rises for energy at today's costs of photovoltaic facilities. What is needed here is a technological breakthrough leading to a considerable reduction in the cost of photovoltaics, in order to make the broad-scale introduction of this energy-supply technology possible.

Hydroelectric power is permanently available at larger rivers; biomass is storable. Both energy sources have therefore found their way into the existing worldwide energy supply picture, or will do so easily in the future.

24 Using Less Energy in the Future

A central module of the future orientation of the worldwide energy supply system is to use as little energy as possible. Here, we will have to make a distinction between savings in the form of less energy consumption by people, and savings by means of technological progress as compared with today's consumption by systems and equipment. Behavior-related reduction potentials are available in the industrialized countries, on the order of magnitude of 10 to 15%. They can be realized immediately; all it takes is the will. On the other hand, technical reduction potentials can be realized only through technological progress and innovative ideas.

Energy technology has made continuous process toward greater energy efficiency for decades. Just within the past forty years, power stations have cut the carbon quantity need to produce a kilowatt-hour of electric power in half. Great untapped reduction potentials are available in the heating of buildings. In the long run, additional insulation and energy rehabilitation of buildings can cut the use of energy for heating in the industrialized countries in half, too. Today, new buildings can already be built at the so-called "three-liter standard," at an acceptable cost. This means that the energy equivalent of only 3 liters of oil (or 3 cu. m. natural gas) is needed per square meter of living space per year. Electrical equipment has also gotten fundamentally thriftier, as have the engines in motor vehicles.

On the other hand, there is expanded demand for energy by consumers, not only in the developing and emerging-market countries, but also in the industrialized countries. The emerging-market countries are trying to follow the same path the industrialized countries, too, have trodden. For this, they need more energy. More energy services are also being demanded in the industrialized countries. The living space to be heated per capita is rising continuously in Germany, the number of electrical devices is increasing, and more kilometers are being driven and flown. This behavior has used up all the savings that technical improvements have brought in recent years. The bottom line is that just as much energy is being consumed as was the case twenty years ago. Energy consumption may be stagnating, but it is not dropping appreciably.

The energy efficiency in power stations, refineries and other energy conversion systems and household equipment is not improving by leaps and bounds, but rather slowly, due to a steady improvement process. Decades will pass before the existing generation of equipment is replaced or buildings are rehabilitated. Changes in the structure of the energy supply system will therefore take a long time. The high degree of bound capital in that system makes short-term radical change impossible for economic reasons.

In spite of all our efforts to manage energy rationally, worldwide primary energy consumption will rise, due to increasing demand from the emerging-market countries of Asia and South America. The necessary thrifty management of energy will mitigate this increase, but will not be able to compensate for it.

25 Cheap Energy Is Running Low

Worldwide energy supply has hitherto essentially been based on energy sources which, expressed in terms of oil prices, can be produced for less than $20 per barrel, or about 9 euro-cents per liter of crude oil. In addition, there are expenditures for the transportation and processing in the refinery. Based on its costs, the product is thus produced for just over 20 cents per liter for the consumer. In 2007, the price without any taxes was about 50 cents per liter. These are the conditions under which the world has to date used its cheap stocks of energy.

The available energy resources are well known. Their extraction is technically possible and, given today's prices of energy, they are marketable. In addition to the "reserves" of energy sources, there are also the so-called "resources." These are deposits which can be extracted only at prohibitive expense, considering the current market price, or else their extraction is not technically possible yet; gas hydrates are an example of the latter category. The figures often published for how long existing energy sources will last, for example forty years for petroleum and sixty years for natural gas, reflect the relationship between known reserves and consumption in a given year; both can change. With price increases and the development of greater technical possibilities for extraction, "resources" become "reserves." The increase in the world's population, energy-efficiency measure and the price levels for energy have in turn affected consumption. The life span of the reserves therefore changes from year to year. It is certain that the resources will in fact be exhausted some day. This will not be the case for oil within the next forty years. At extraction costs in the area of $20 to $40 per barrel, or a doubling over today's extraction costs, many times as many energy reserves as what has been consumed to date will become available. The oil sands in Canada are an example.

What these considerations mean is that the extraction costs and hence the market prices for the energy sources in the future, will get more expensive.

The energy resources are distributed unevenly throughout the world. While hard coal is available on all continents, petroleum deposits are concentrated in the Middle East and in South and Central America. Some 70% of today's known worldwide natural-gas reserves are located in the strategic belt between Siberia, the Caspian Sea and the Middle East. On the other hand, uranium deposits and renewable energy sources are scattered across the world.

Besides the quantity question, there is also the question of political access to energy. Major deposits of petroleum are located in Muslim countries. In the longer run, economic rationality applies to them, too. They must gain foreign exchange from oil sales to keep their economies going. Nevertheless, it has been shown repeatedly in the past that they will diverge from this path of economic rationality for political reasons at short notice. The security of the energy supply is therefore one of the major issues of the next decades. The meaning of the word "security" can be expanded beyond that of mere quantitative availability. The interruption of the supply of energy is a conceivable objective of criminal and terrorist actions. A secure energy supply requires worldwide dialogue; we are only at the beginning of it.

26 A Look to the Future

What does the picture of our future energy supply look like for the next twenty to forty years? The energy sources coal, oil and natural gas will continue to account for a substantial share of the future energy-supply picture; they will be supplemented by nuclear power in some countries. Renewable energies will be increasingly and steadily introduced into the energy-supply mix in many countries. Moreover, in the long run the rising prices of energy will promote energy savings and particularly energy efficiency in equipment. There will, however, also be conflicts over the goals of future energy supply. For example, the separation of carbon dioxide for reasons of climate protection will lead to a decline in the energy efficiency of power stations. The successes in energy efficiency increase of the past thirty years will largely be nullified in this area.

We face the ethical necessity to make every effort to further limit the disequilibrium in worldwide energy consumption. For that purpose, measures aimed at restricting the increase in the prices of energy are necessary, particularly energy-saving measures, such as more efficient energy conversion, and also the tapping of new energy sources. Only in this way can prices be such that poor countries, too, will have conditional access to energy on the world markets.

Technically speaking, there are many options under development which can be incorporated into the future energy-supply structure. Hydrogen fuel cells will be able to produce electric power and heat in a decentralized manner, for example; the hydrogen can be obtained by splitting water with electric power from nuclear power stations or renewable sources, and then stored. The potentials for the use of deep geothermal energy can be opened up.

The question for the future is not: "is humankind running out of energy?" – to which the answer would be "Yes, we are running out of cheap and easily available energy, but not expensive energy." The two central questions for the future are rather: "How can we reduce the disequilibrium in energy consumption between the industrial and the developing countries, and hence the disparity in standards of living?" and "How can we make it economically possible to pay considerably more for energy in the long run?"

The industrialized nations have many possibilities and options for using energy sources and improving energy technology. Also, the potentials for reductions in all countries are still far from exhausted. Due to limited domestic energy resources, the European Union is forced to buy the major share of its energy on the world market. Its energy supply is therefore tied to world events. At the same time, it is pursuing ambitious goals, in terms of climate-protection and air-pollutant-reduction targets. The energy-supply system of the future must therefore be oriented in as balanced a manner as possible toward

– a sufficiently secure energy supply
– affordable energy prices which support the competitiveness of business
– an energy supply friendly to the climate and to the environment, and
– use of energy sources acceptable to the people.

This will require a permanent discussion and decision-making process. In view of the existing long-term uncertainties, that energy-supply system which leaves open as many options as possible will be the best one. Concretely, this requires the use of all energy sources, a further increase in energy efficiency and of consciousness of energy-saving, as well as a permanent dialogue between decision-makers and the people about the facts and the future orientation of energy supply. The development and introduction to the market of as many innovative energy technologies as possible is imperative. This will require increased research and development efforts and good education and training.

The future of energy supply is a challenge. We cannot escape this challenge. However, we are well equipped to meet it. All we have to do is to want to do so.

Glossary

Barrel	Measurement unit for petroleum: 1 barrel = 159 liters.
Biological oxidation	Power generation by the gradual oxidization of high-energy, organic compounds.
Biomass	The natural material of vegetable and animal organisms, which is continually newly formed in the hydrocarbon cycle.
Carbon dioxide (CO$_2$)	Colorless, nontoxic, non-combustible gas produced by exhalation and by the combustion of energy source containing carbon. It is an important greenhouse gas.
Carbon monoxide (CO)	Colorless, odorless, toxic gas, formed by the combustion of substances containing carbon, with an inadequate oxygen supply.
Carbonization gas	Gasses produced at high temperatures but without access to air, e.g. in the production of charcoal.
Cogeneration (CHP)	The cogeneration of heat and power, which provides process heat for industry and district heat for heating, saves up to 15% of the energy produced, compared with the separate production of electric power and heat.
Condensation energy	Heat liberated when steam liquefies to water by cooling down.
Crude oil	Petroleum in the form it has when it is extracted to the earth's surface. It is a complex mixture of various hydrocarbons, the composition and characteristics of which depend on its origin.
Degree of effectiveness	Ratio of the energy quantity generated (output) by a conversion system (power station, boiler) to the energy quantity (input) used. It is always less than 100%.

Deregulation   In a deregulated energy market, there is no monopoly by
                          companies for a certain industry, such as electric power
                          or gas. Customers can buy their energy from whichever
                          company they like best. Grid operators (electric cables,
                          pipelines) must pass the energy through for a fee.

Duration time   Wind and solar energy facilities produce electric
                          power unevenly over the course of the year, due to its
                          availability. Utilization time is the fictitious figure for the
                          number of hours which the system would have to run
                          constantly at maximum output to produce its annual
                          power output. In Germany, that value for photovoltaics
                          facilities is a maximum of 1000 hours; for onshore wind
                          systems, it is between 1600 and 2200 hours, for offshore,
                          about 4000 hours.

Electrolysis of water   The splitting of water into hydrogen and oxygen by
                          means of electrical energy.

Emissions   The ejection of air-polluting substances or greenhouse
                          gasses into the atmosphere.

End-use energy   Energy used by consumers to meet their energy
                          requirements (households, industry, trade, services).

Energy commodity   The trade in electricity and gas on a commodities
trading   exchange. In the decontrolled market, ever more
                          quantities of grid-bound energies are being traded on the
                          exchange.

Energy efficiency   Collective term for all technical measures for the
                          improvement of energy conversion. The higher energy
                          efficiency is, the less coal per kilowatt-hour of electricity
                          will have to be used, e.g., in a power station, or the
                          mpg of vehicle are higher. Instead of energy efficiency,
                          the concept "efficient energy use" or "efficient energy
                          transformation" is also frequently used.

Energy source   Term in daily usage, which can mean a primary energy
                          source, but also a secondary or end-use energy. Even
                          energy saving is frequently described as an energy
                          source.

Energy services	Consumer needs for energy, such as rooms at a comfortable temperature, information, etc., which can be met by the use of energy sources.
Energy stock	All known and suspected primary energy deposits, subdivided into "reserves" and "resources" (see above).
Fermentation	Transformation of biological materials with the help of bacteria, mushroom or cell cultures. If this is done in the absence of oxygen, it is called anaerobic fermentation.
Fossil energy sources	Coal, oil and gas; they produce various amounts of carbon dioxide (CO_2) when burned.
Fusion	The process whereby the nuclei of the lightest atom, hydrogen, are fused to form slightly heavier helium nuclei, thus generating energy.
Geothermal energy	The heat of the earth's crust, which increases by about 30°C per kilometer of depth. These are also are hot-water deposits and super-hot rocks in the earth.
Greenhouse effect	Caused by gasses such as carbon dioxide or steam, which let short-wave solar radiation through to the earth's surface almost unhindered, but strongly absorb the long-wave thermal radiation reflected back from the earth's surface and the lower layers of the atmosphere. The burning of coal, oil and natural gas has produced additional carbon dioxide, which has this effect and causes the temperature of the atmosphere to rise.
Gross national product (GNP)	The monetary value of all goods and services consumed, invested or exported by a national economy in a year, minus imports. Identical with the income of the national economy.
Heating gas	Collective term for hot combustion gasses which heat up water or air over a heat exchanger. Fossil energy sources or biomass but also waste can be burned.
Heating value	The energy quantity released by oil and gas as heat during combustion, without taking into account the condensation heat of the steam reconverted to water.
High-temperature reactor	Nuclear reactor moderated not by water but by graphite, so that it can produce higher steam temperatures than other reactor types.

Hydrogen fuel cells	Device which catalytically "burns" hydrogen (either pure or in the form of fuels containing hydrogen) with atmospheric oxygen, and thus produces electric power.
Isotope	Naturally occurring or artificially produced radioactive atoms. Isotope disintegration turns it into a different chemical element.
Light water reactor (LWR)	Nuclear power station which uses water as a moderator and at the same time as a coolant. It is the most common nuclear-reactor type worldwide.
Limited partner	Financial associate of a company not tied into the management. Onshore wind parks are financed by limited-partnership companies.
Monopoly	The market dominating position of a supplier or a group closed of suppliers. One talks about partial monopoly if few suppliers pursue a coordinated delivering policy.
Natural gas	Primarily methane (CH_4), a hydrocarbon molecule consisting of one carbon atom and four hydrogen atoms which is gaseous under normal conditions.
Nuclear fission	The splitting of heavy atomic nuclei, such as those of uranium, to generate nuclear energy.
OECD-IEA	The Organization for Economic Cooperation and Development (OECD) is the organization of the industrialized countries. It runs the International Energy Agency (IEA), which is responsible for crisis management should an energy shortage occur; it also observes and analyzes the international energy market.
OPEC	Organization of Petroleum Exporting Countries, founded in 1960, based in Vienna. The OPEC countries have huge quantities of oil which are cheap to extract.
Perpetual-motion machine	General term for a theoretical engine which would run with no added energy. According to the laws of physics, this is not possible.
Photolysis	Procedure in basic research by means of which water is split directly into hydrogen and oxygen by sunlight.
Photo-oxidants	Chemical air pollutants, e.g. ozone, created from precursors in the atmosphere under the effect of sunlight.

Photovoltaic (solar) cells	Thin semiconductor layers, often silicon-based, into which light is absorbed and converted directly into electrical energy. Silicon-based PVs are distinguished by their crystalline form as either monocrystalline, multicrystalline or amorphous.
Primary energy source	An energy source in the original form provided by nature and not treated by humans yet. We distinguish between fossil, nuclear and regenerative primary energy sources.
Primary recovery	Oil production method under which a hole is drilled to a deposit and the oil is forced to the earth's surface by the pressure of the earth's crust above the deposit. This method can extract only approximately a quarter of the oil in the deposit.
Reserves	That portion of energy stocks which has been located precisely and can be extracted economically with existing technology.
Reserves/production ratio	Ratio of reserves to consumption for a given energy source at a given point in time.
Resources	That portion of energy stocks which is either proven or suspected geologically, but the extraction of which is not yet technically and/or economically feasible.
Secondary recovery	Oil production method under which additional pressure is created in the deposit by pumping in steam or CO_2. In this way, the degree of oil extraction can be increased.
Solar-thermal collectors	Mostly flat collectors which absorb sunlight to a high degree and turn it into usable heat of up to 90°C.
Solar-thermal power station	Power station, usually in the earth's equatorial sun belt, in which sunlight shining directly onto a large area of minors is concentrated onto a heat absorber by focusing mirrors. The heat, between 400 and 700°, drives a power station process.
Spot market	A trading center, of which a few trade oil; prices change almost hourly.
Sulfur dioxide (SO₂)	Colorless polluting gas with a piercing smell which is e.g. released in the combustion of sulfurous fuels (coal, petroleum, biomass).

Tertiary recovery   See secondary recovery: in addition, chemicals are
                         injected into the deposit to reduce the viscosity of the
                         oil and enable a degree of extraction beyond secondary
                         recovery possibilities.

Transformation   System by which different forms of biomass are
system   converted into gasses or liquid energy sources on a
                         chemical, biological way.

Uranium (U-235 &   The heaviest atomic element which occurs naturally on
U-238)   earth; it is radioactive, its consist of ninety-two protons
                         and 143 (U-235) or 146 neutrons (U-238) neutrons.
                         Natural uranium contains 99.3% U-235 and 0.7%
                         U-238. U-235 is used as a nuclear fuel in nuclear reactors.

Bibliography

Chapter 2

Tatyana P. Soubbotina: *Beyond Economic Growth – An Introduction to Sustainable Development*, 2nd edition, The World Bank, Washington, D.C., 2004

Report of the World Bank which addresses the questions of the worldwide disequilibrium of incomes. In addition to statistical data, it contains a large number of considerations for the support of the poor countries.

Chapter 7

J. Mathur, H.-J. Wagner, N.K. Bansal: *Energy Security, Climate Change and Sustainable Development*, Anarnaya Publishes, New Dehli, 2007. The book contains a number of contributions by various different authors. T.J. Petrovic & H.-J. Wagner, in "How Sustainable Are Renewable Energy Systems?", describe the choice and application of indicators for the assessment of various sources of energy.

Chapter 8

Klaus Heinloth: *Die Energiefrage* (The Energy Issue – in German), Viehweg-Verlag, Brunswick/Wiesbaden, 2nd printing, 2003. This account addresses the question as to how future energy needs can be met. Starting from the existing situation, it describes the technical and physical possibilities and potentials of particular power options, and at the end arrives at a scenario for future energy-supply requirements. The author works through the questions quantitatively in a physical/ technical approach.

Illustrations

All graphics: Peter Palm, Berlin